SKID ROW

By
William McSheehy

G.K.HALL&CO.

70 LINCOLN STREET, BOSTON, MASS.

Schenkman Publishing Company
Cambridge, Massachusetts

Copyright © 1979 by Schenkman Publishing Company, Inc.

Library of Congress Cataloging in Publication Data

McSheehy, William.
   Skid Row.

   Bibliography: p.
   Includes index.
   1.   Tramps — Illinois — Chicago.   2.   Chicago — Poor.
   3.   Chicago — Social conditions.   4.   Subculture.
I.   Title.
HV4506 C5M3   301.2′2   78-11462
ISBN 0-8161-9008-9
ISBN 0-87073-181-5 pbk.

This publication is printed on permanent/durable acid-free paper
MANUFACTURED IN THE UNITED STATES OF AMERICA

Contents

Acknowledgements

I must acknowledge a debt of gratitude to the many men of Skid Row who participated in this study. In particular I thank Howard Church, Lorenzo Young Eagle, and Harry Cralle for their time, thoughts, and friendship.

I am grateful to Dr. Lauren Langman, Elizabeth Freidheim, Dr. Dancuole Variakojis, and especially Dr. Thomas Gannon, S. J. for their suggestions which did much to improve the manuscript. I should also like to thank editor Libby Koponen and Schenkman Publishing Co. for valuable comments. I am most indebted to my wife, Margaret, who gave unselfishly of her help throughout the research and writing of the book.

Finally, I would like to thank my family for their interest and support.

Introduction

The primary interest in this study is not with the men of Skid Row. Many other studies have dealt with them. Rather, my concern is with the institutions which sustain the subculture of Skid Row. I will attempt to demonstrate how major institutions foster Skid Row's existence.

An important function of Skid Row is to reinforce values necessary for maintaining the American capitalistic system. In this society where only a few may attain important positions of authority, power, and prestige, and some people must scrub floors and toilets, prejudices evolve both to justify the disequilibrium that exists between rich and poor and to preserve the prevailing socio-economic order. Thus, Skid Row bums are regarded not only as "failures" but as morally degenerate and emotionally disturbed. A major underlying argument of this monograph is that this belief becomes a rationale which tolerates the exploitation of these men and promotes work and success ethics.

For many people in the United States, Skid Row[1] is that section of a city experienced only from a moving automobile with doors locked and windows closed. The usual interests are derelicts lying drunk and passed out on the sidewalks and bums wearing shabby old clothes which give the impression that they have not been washed or cleaned in years. To many persons unfamiliar with this urban culture a Skid Row is something of a leper colony. These sensational and superficial concerns often encourage misunderstanding.

Skid Rows are those areas in most major cities in the United States characterized by bars, temporary employment agencies, grills, rescue missions, and cheap hotels. Skid Rows did not come

1

into existence in this country until a little over one hundred years ago. Located along the Great Lakes and in the midwest, Chicago became a major railroad center and an important port for the shipping industry in the years following the Civil War. The rapid settlement of the frontier resulted in the West sending food and animal products by rail to the East and importing manufactured products in exchange. Railroad lines were built north, west and south from Chicago into rich lumber and farming areas. The Chicago River served as the principal harbor and an important area of commerce for the city. The dock frontage along the river was crowded with grain elevators, coal yards, steel mills, manufacturing industries and warehouses. All the train systems had terminals along the river and its branches.

Chicago was the largest market in the United States for the casual and seasonal worker. Men who worked seasonal jobs like harvesting crops would in off seasons search for work at the many employment offices on Skid Row. Madison Street, South State Street, and North Clark Street, with their saloons and inexpensive lodging and eating places, attracted many men who came to Chicago looking for work as gandy dancers, lumberjacks, dock workers, or migrant seasonal workers (Anderson, 1923).

From the late 1890s to the early 1900s on the near west side—particularly West Madison Street—and in the "Levee District" of the First Ward which included South State Street, there flourished numerous gambling halls, barrel-houses, pawn shops, brothels, and concert saloons. For the man with money, the barrel-house combined a rooming house, saloon, house of prostitution and gambling hall under one roof. The barrel-houses were named because of the liquor drawn from barrels along the four walls of the saloons.

A general depression in the early 1890's caused extensive unemployment. Chicago became overrun with the jobless, and City Hall opened its doors each night for one thousand five hundred of these men to sleep in its corridors. Many of Skid Row's hungry jobless depended for their food on saloons which offered free lunches and, if they had a nickel, a glass of beer. Michael "Hinky Dink" Kenna, the infamous cigar chewing alderman of the First Ward, owned such a saloon, "The Working Man's Exchange", on

2

Clark Street south of Van Buren, where for years he fed bums and tramps. Above his saloon was a flophouse which accommodated three hundred men, and during elections twice as many—(Wendt and Kogan, 1943; Longstreet, 1973).

In 1894 many of those without jobs in Chicago went off and joined Jacob Coxey's army and marched to Washington to support legislation to create jobs for the thousands of unemployed in the country. When they reached Washington they were repulsed by police who clubbed many of them. Coxey was arrested before he was able to read his speech and was put in jail for trespassing on Capitol grounds.

About 1900, many lofts and warehouses were converted into cubicle hotels. In 1911 an estimated 40,000 to 60,000 men lived on Chicago's Skid Rows (Solenberger 1911). The number of men increased greatly during periods of high unemployment such as after World War I and the depression of the 1930's. Following the First World War it was no longer possible to obtain the free lunch and five cent schooner of beer. The concert saloons with their dancing, open gambling and female services also disappeared (Anderson, 1940).

The economic prosperity and government work programs of the 1940s reduced considerably the population of Skid Row. With the prosperous years following World War II the number of inhabitants on Chicago's Skid Rows began to decline steadily. A survey made in 1957 found a total of 11,926 men living in Skid Row areas of the city. As of 1978, the entire West Madison Street Skid Row has been almost completely demolished by Urban Renewal projects.[2]

Notes

[1]The term skid row is derived from "skid road", the name for a center of logging activities. It was down this thoroughfare that the logs were skidded to the sawmills. Dilapidated hotels, saloons and gambling houses were built along the skid road for the lumberjacks. Over the years the term grew to include not only these areas but also those areas inhabited by other transient men.

[2]Most of the research for this book was completed by 1974.

Chapter I

Skid Row Areas

To define Skid Row only in terms of physical area, demography, or social pathology is representative largely of shallow thought processes (for example, Vanderkooi, 1968:23). This would relegate a complex system of behavior, attitudes, values and norms to a symptomatic formula; it is as much to understand an effect as the cause. Assuming that Skid Row is a culture[1] of urban man, we are confronted by the question, can any one culture be defined? Though a definition here is unlikely, there are traits and conditions capable of being described and analyzed, that govern the existence of Skid Row and distinguish it from other subcultures.

Three integral reasons dictate the existence of Skid Row. These are 1) the industrial society with its endemic problems, 2) individuals who are unable to adapt "successfully" to the economic system of this society, and 3) the different agencies which have evolved to administer to the needs and wants of those beset by marginal situations.

Factors responsible for the emergence of Skid Row were the growth of industrialization and urbanization. Changes in the economic system had wide ramifications on the structures of society, among which were the displacement of agricultural workers from the farm, and obsolescence and/or insufficient knowledge of skills and values associated with technology. Therefore, while most people acquired the values and skills necessary for adaptation to the emergent industrialization, many did not. To be sure, many of these "skills" were minimal. Perhaps more important were the

5

values such as punctuality, regularity, and obedience to superiors. One result of industrialization was thus the emergence of a minority without subsistence resources or the values and skills requisite to the attainment of these resources.

Physical area is an important determinant of Skid Row. What is it, then, about the physical area that can qualify this statement? In other words, what is it that differentiates Skid Row areas from other areas? Briefly it is the institutions: the bars, short-order restaurants, missions, day labor offices, second-hand stores, hotels, and apartment rooms, which serve the needs of those individuals who gravitate to Skid Row areas.

There are, however, bars, grills, and apartment rooms, which charge prices no different than those on Skid Row, located throughout much of the social strata in the United States. Second-hand stores (or resale stores), store-front missions and day labor offices are not unknown to other poor sections of cities. The store-front missions in poor, usually black, neighborhoods are unlike Skid Row missions in that the former are more family-established, and do not generally have to seduce the poor into becoming, for want of a meal, their hapless congregation. Further, "Negro store-front churces of Chicago are clearly far removed from the staid and stolid Puritanism that has dominated the American Protestant tradition" (Keil, 1966:8).

The most distinguishing Skid Row institutions are the $1.50 to $2.00 per night transient hotels and the "soup and salvation" missions. Nowhere else except Skid Rows do these exist so prominently. Flophouses, missions, and in part the day labor offices, are undoubtedly the major deciding institutions of a Skid Row. There are multiple reasons for this, but to summarize, they help foster an important nomadic aspect of this subculture. Where else can so many men "flop" for less than $1.50? A man with no money need only seek refuge at a mission or work day labor. Thus these institutions offer an alternative to that portion of Skid Row men who are indisposed toward the "normal" exigencies of life. The phenomenon of Chicago's Skid Row is not due specifically to any one of these institutions in and of itself; instead it is/was the unique combination and frequency of these institutions within an area.

6

Skid Row may be understood as complicated and intricate systems of interaction among its inhabitants. Some of these systems are more formal or institutionalized and lend themselves to observation. Institutions must realize some goal; for business institutions, those economically motivated, the goal is profit, at least insofar as profit is needed to pay one's debts. In order for any such agency to exist it must address its operations to the physical and/or emotional needs of its customers. Thus, the existence of Skid Row institutions is ultimately rooted in the needs of this cultural group. This fact accounts for the disproportionate representation of certain types of institutions already mentioned: bars, day labor offices, etc., and explains why Skid Row has a noticeable absence of retail establishments ordinary to most other communities: bakeries, cleaners, 5 & 10 stores, bowling alleys, department stores, ice cream parlors, super markets, sporting goods stores, florists, hobby shops, etc. (see maps)

Skid Row agencies can be seen as analogous to botanical organisms competing within an ecological niche where only a limited number of those species most successfully adapted can exist. Given a definite population of potential clients with special needs and substandard income, only a limited number of agencies can survive. As of 1972, there were, on the fifteen block area of Madison Street, forty-one bars, twenty-one day labor offices, twenty-five missions, one barber college, thirteen short-order restaurants (grills), twenty hotels, eleven second-hand and three clothing stores. If these institutions are reliable approximations of the men's needs, then the important needs of Skid Row men are inexpensive food, shelter and clothing, temporary work, alcohol and/or the social/emotional needs associated with them.

Skid Row Related Areas

The areas surrounding West Madison Street frequented by men from Skid Row must be understood as consequences of these institutions. Several of these merit attention. Survival strategies on Skid Row are as varied as its participants. A place to sleep or a means of getting food is limited only by the imagination of a Skid

West Madison Street

West Madison Street

A truck lot north of West Madison Street

In warm weather Skid Row men live inside many of these trucks.

Rower. Some strategies, through wide usage, become culturally patterned. The Northwestern Train Station, for example, is at Clinton and Madison Streets. A few Skid Row men panhandle the workaday commuters at its entrances. In the extremes of winter, when a Skid Row man is too tired, weak and/or cold to "carry the banner" (walk the street all night), without the assets for a hotel room or too late for the missions, he may steal himself into the warmth and security of a bench or telephone booth inside the station. North of Madison Street on Milwaukee Avenue and Kinzie (400 north) are the "Indian Docks." Here there are abandoned loading docks which are the Skid Row Indians' "municipal" flop. East of the docks, in the area immediately south of Kinzie Street, there is a freight train yard. Just South of this (north of Carrol Street, 334 north) there are lots strewn with truck trailers, many of which have fallen into disuse. Men who find sleeping (on papers, cardboard, blankets or an old mattress) in one of the vans compatible with a life on Skid Row sojourn here especially in the summer. Two blocks north of Madison Street on Randolf Street, and a few blocks

Skid Row men often go through the garbage of the Randolf Street markets to find something to eat.

11

east of the Kennedy Expressway, is Chicago's major wholesale produce market. Today there are a few weathered "tramps" who will search refuse boxes in order to retrieve perishable items like fruits or vegetables which have approached a rather undesirable stage in the carbon cycle. Many times by cutting off a decayed part, one or more men can salvage enough to throw into a large can and make a mulligan stew.

What separates the geography of Skid Row from that of other areas is not an abrupt transition but a continuum with Madison Street, Clark Street, State Street, etc., as its foci. If by rough calculation Skid Rows were only those areas which accommodate certain types of individuals, then Skid Row would not be limited to areas such as Madison Street. Parks, hospitals, boxcars, highways, factories, farms, depots, old buildings, ad infinitum, while not unknown to most Skid Row men, aren't usually thought of as Skid Row areas.

Other Businesses on Skid Row

An often neglected fact is that Skid Row is not composed of just flophouses, day labor offices, bars, etc. (see maps). There are many other types of businesses which operate here and have neither direct dependence on Skid Row itself nor contribute to its maintenance. Madison Street Skid Row has a large concentration of store fixture businesses, many of which have existed in this area for over forty years. In the 1920's Madison Street was the store fixture center in Chicago. Skid Row men do not prove adequate patrons for these businessmen. Yet their continued presence in the area bears evidence that Skid Row does not greatly impede their operations. Rent in this area is cheap. It is next to the loop and easily accessible from the Kennedy Expressway. Skid Row doesn't discourage potential customers at these stores, since the majority of business comes from old customers, referrals, or contracts based on architect's blueprints. The store merchants don't object to Skid Row because as one of the owners puts it, ''The bums keep pretty much to themselves and don't bother us.''

The gracious Mid City Bank and Holiday Inn (which one informant described as "the sore thumb of Skid Row") are also present there, though owners, managers and personnel hardly hobnob with the men on Skid Row.

Other Skid Row Areas

A comparative analysis of Skid Rows throughout Chicago yields this information: the Madison Street area is decidedly the largest. Madison Street Skid Row is located one block west of Chicago's central business district. It occupies the area along Madison Street from 600 west to 1600 west and one block north and three blocks south of Madison at Halsted. There are also Skid Row buildings used by habitues of that street, situated on north and south side

A park on the west bank of the Chicago River between Washington and Randolf Streets where some Skid Row men sleep on summer nights

streets extending in some cases up to four blocks from Madison. Further, there is that part of Skid Row which extends beyond the Madison area in discussion, i.e., many men, regulars to Madison Street Skid Row, have their apartments or apartment rooms throughout the city, and periodically, when seized by lonliness, visit Skid Row.

In addition to Madison Street Skid Row, there are four other Skid Row areas in Chicago: South State Street, North Clark Street, Milwaukee and Division, and Broadway and Wilson.

(1) South State Street Skid Row: from Roosevelt Road (1200 south) north to VanBuren (400 south), west on VanBuren to Clark Street, and one block south. This was once a thriving Skid Row area, although now only a few vestigal buildings remain. There are two day labor offices, one very large mission used by many Skid Rowers from Madison, and nine hotels in the South State area, accommodating approximately one thousand individuals. The population of the five cubicle hotels in this area is almost nine hundred.

TABLE 1.1 CHICAGO SKID ROWS
BY INSTITUTIONS

	Madison Street	South State Street	North Clark Street	Milwaukee and Division	Uptown Skid Row Area
Missions	25	1	2	1	1
Day Labor Offices	21	2	2	1	11
Hotels	20	9	5	1	2

(2) North Clark Street Skid Row: from Kinzie (400 north) to Chicago Avenue (800 north). Most of this has already been torn down by urban renewal projects. North Clark had two day labor offices, five hotels (none cubicle) housing a total of 354 men, and two rather small "soup line" missions.

14

(3) Milwaukee and Division Skid Row: on Milwaukee south of Division and west two blocks along Division. This is a Skid Row perhaps only in the widest possible understanding. There is one large hotel (transients; $6.75 per night), one small mission, and one day labor office.

(4) Broadway and Wilson Skid Row: from Montrose (440 north) along Broadway to Leland (4700 North), and along Sheridan Road (1000 west) to Wilson Avenue (4600 north); from Sheridan Road three blocks west along Wilson to Broadway, and one block west of Broadway on Wilson. The most striking feature of this Uptown area is the number of day labor offices. There are also institutions reminiscent of Skid Row: one large mission serving up to seventy "unattached" men per day, and two flophouses (one large $2.00 per night cubicle hotel, and one small $3.00 per night room hotel; both were built almost fifty years ago). Aside from this lodging there are rundown hotels and apartment rooms throughout Uptown.

The Outcome

Skid Row does not introduce problems to the dominant society. The institutions which comprise Skid Row reflect the particularistic needs of its inhabitants. Thus, as Skid Row's buildings are demolished, Skid Row as such will not be eliminated, but merely altered. A general misconception holds that because buildings are razed on Madison Street, this conversely necessitates that all the men and agencies are uniformly redistributed to other Skid Row areas, eventually expanding them to the magnitude of the original area. Although this opinion has some application in truth, it tends to beg proper analysis, and ultimately is misleading.

Reasons why Madison Skid Row is not relocating *en masse* to other Skid Row areas in the city are: 1) city ordinances passed in the last thirty years, and rising expenses, have prohibited the construction of hotels with 5' X 7' rooms and wire mesh ceilings; 2) all the present Skid Rows date back at least forty to fifty years; and 3) Urban Renewal has been executing programs in all of the present Skid Rows.

Areas to which the men will be forced to migrate must meet the basic needs of this group. These needs may be met by the existent institutions of poor areas, such as inexpensive hotels and apartment rooms instead of the vermin-ridden cubicle hotels, etc.

It is important to remember that many inhabitants of West Madison Street were familiar with other Skid Row areas in Chicago. There are many reasons for this. The following are a few: 1) missions offering nightly shelter have a policy that new arrivals have first rights to beds; fervid beneficiaries are the least likely to qualify. In result, some men rotate their attendance at these missions to diminish their chances of being turned away; 2) most Skid Row Indians occasionally go to the Uptown Broadway Skid Row to get an apartment room or stay with a friend or relative, or just to imbibe at taverns like the Crazy Horse, TeePee, and Reservation; 3) a resident may leave Madison Street to avoid trouble. If a man jackrolls some money from an associate, he can disappear with the inheritance for a few days or weeks and thereby bypass the initial wrath of the victim; 4) some men may depart from Madison Street to other Skid Rows just as a relief from boredom.

Summary

There are three factors responsible for the existence of Skid Rows in the United States: 1) the industrial economic system with its problems, 2) the inability of some individuals to "successfully" adapt to this system, and 3) the Skid Row institutions (flophouses, day labor offices, and rescue missions) which attract those individuals with insufficient economic resources.

Madison Street remains the largest Skid Row in Chicago. Other important Skid Row areas are South State and North Clark. These Skid Row areas are presently being torn down. Consequently, the men who live there are forced to relocate in other areas of the city.

Notes

[1]Skid Row is taken as a subculture in that the human needs of its inhabitants are supplemented by distinct interaction forms (learned behavior patterns, etc.) which enable men to adapt to this urban environment.

Chapter II

The Missions of Skid Row

Social stratification, the differential allocation of income and prestige based on one's life chances, is an integral part of industrial society; the differential distributions of these life chances render some groups and individuals "successful" in terms of adaptation to the dominant social system. Some groups and individuals are less successful and may, of necessity, be socialized into the values and norms of Skid Row culture.[1]

Social institutions and agencies (missions, hotels, bars, second-hand stores, grills, police) have evolved to administer to the needs and wants of those individuals undergoing marginal situations. These institutions, in point of fact, are largely responsible for perpetuating the existence of Skid Row. The Skid Row mission is one such institution with an extreme disparity between its manifest and latent functions. While the missions purportedly aim to "rehabilitate" the indigenous Skid Row population and ameliorate the conditions, they are in fact central to the maintenance of this urban culture.

The Skid Row mission must be understood in terms of historical influences, the types of persons who become missionaries, the organization of the missions, and finally the effects these missions have on Skid Row.

The Skid Row mission, a product of the "Protestant Ethic" and Western industrialization, is an anachronism rooted in late nineteenth century United States history.

These missions first marshalled their tidy doctrines to the Skid

Row cause in the post Civil War days, when they were founded to "cater to the needy slum families as well as the unattached homeless . . ." (Wallace, 1968:51). The early Skid Row missions served as the major agencies providing relief to those persons existing on a hand to mouth basis. In the face of these conditions, political sentiment, then as at the present, was somewhat indifferent, if not hostile, to the needs of Skid Rowers. Since governmental help was minimal or nonexistent, the missions did in fact provide some useful services. The motivating purpose of these missions, however, was evangelical rather than simply the provision of food and shelter.

The Origins of the Missions

In order to understand the Skid Row mission, one must consider its antecedent factors. The "Protestant Ethic" of hard work and asceticism gave a moral evaluation to one's work. The doctrine of predestination evoked anxiety about one's status as saved or damned. Economic success became an indication of having attained grace, failure was regarded as evidence of sin. Early writers deplored the impoverished, the beggars, and the vanquished. Howard James, writing in 1868, stated:

Perchance it may be our good fortune to gain a few converts to the cause of true humanity—an absolute repudiation of beggars: perhaps we may contribute something to the growth of that wholesome feeling which points to the encouragement of honest industry as the first duty of a good citizen, and to indiscriminate almsgiving as a folly and a sin (James, 1868:4).

While sociologists have long considered the "Protestant Ethic" as a normative code legitimizing achievement orientations, we must also remember the evangelical aspects of Protestantism. Sociologically, a sect differs from a church in that a sect is self-established and/or solicited; one is born into a church. Thus, fundamentalist sects, particularly those more prevalent in rural or low income strata, are especially likely to engage in evangelical proselytizing. Their theologies are likely to include concrete emotional

18

expressions and explanations which are usually based on literal interpretations of the Bible.

The Missionaries

Table 2.1 presents the demographic characteristics of the directors of the Chicago (West Madison Street vicinity) Skid Row missions. The modal pattern shows that the typical mission director is a rural born, white Protestant male, over fifty, married and with children. His father was either a semi-skilled worker, a farmer, or a preacher. Unless he is under thirty-five (less than one in five) he did not finish high school. This rural background predisposes one to regard urban conditions as aberrations from a pastoral norm. The mission directors' limited levels of education in addition to their evangelical orientation preclude abstract "explanations" for Skid Row, such as a limited opportunity structure or technologically induced marginality.

TABLE 2.1 THE MISSION DIRECTORS
AND ASSISTANT DIRECTORS*

	Per Cent	Number
Age		
20-30	17	4
30-40	0	0
40-50	8	2
50-60	46	11
60-70	29	7
Place of Birth, Age 20-35		
Foreign	0	0
Rural America	75	3
Urban America	25	1
Place of Birth, Age 45-70		
Foreign	35	7
Rural America	55	11
Urban America	10	2
Childhood Religion		
Catholic	12	3
Protestant	87	21
Marital Status		
Married	96	23
With Children	87	21
Unmarried	4	1

Father's Occupation		
Semi-Skilled Laborer	50	12
Farmer	21	5
Preacher	29	7
Education, Age 20-35		
Completed Grammar School	—	—
Some High School	—	—
Completed High School	—	—
Religious College	100	4
Education, Age 35-70		
Completed Grammar School	10	2
Some High School	40	8
Completed High School	35	7
Religious College	15	3
Special Training, Age 20-35		
Religious**	100	4
Full-time	—	—
Converts from Skid Row	—	—
Special Training, Age 45-70		
Religious**	63	12
Full-time	21	4
Converts from Skid Row	16	3

*The Catholic and Episcopal directors and assistants are not included in these figures since they do not engage in evangelical proselytization.
**Those with religious training usually had part-time semi-skilled jobs before entering the ministry.

The mission directors have vested interests in failure. If, theoretically, they were successful in terminating this subculture, they would lose their clients, and with them their jobs which often pay about $10,000 a year and may include a car. With rather limited credentials there is little chance that many of these directors would be seeking more suitable employment. An eighth of the older directors were themselves "converts" from the street; there is some evidence that embracing Christ can bring salvation, grace and a comparatively satisfying income.

Admittedly, many of these Skid Row preachers are quite sincere in their conviction and devotion to their religious beliefs, but only therewith follows their incessant zeal to help the poor.

To transmit a doctrine, be it religion or revolution, poetry or politics, one must have an audience. For evangelical fundamentalism, Skid Row offers an optimal environment. The Skid Row missions readily interpret physical deprivation as an index of spiritual deviation. Not only were the men "fallen" sinners in need of the "divine message," but without resources they often had no place to go in order to obtain food, shelter and clothes. Such a group becomes a captive following for the evangelical ministry whose basic values emphasize hard work and "acceptance of the Lord" as virtues; laziness and indulgence are cardinal sins. Only the elect warrant salvation. Skid Row missionaries, when asked, "What do you feel is the most significant reason why men are on Skid Row?", without exception attributed this condition to sin. A preacher at Chicago United Mission commented, "Skid Row's basic corruption is sin—that's the nature of man. You leave a man to himself and he goes downhill; drink, sex, dope are the fruits of sin." And where there is sin, the voice of God is not far away. The residents of Skid Row are ideally suited for "conversion." They are "sinners" who are in large measure dependent on the missions for survival. Attendance at mission services is a prerequisite for any individual to qualify as a recipient of the various types of mission assistance.

As long as explanations for Skid Row are based on personal immorality, the missions serve a function. Evangelical religion has generally focussed on individual transformation rather than social action. Peter Berger (1961) has argued that evangelical fundamentalism, by preoccupation with personal sin, usually of a sexual nature, rather than social justice, "unintentionally" contributed to the maintenance of racial segregation. In the same way, the Skid Row mission, with its ideology of spiritual misfortune, offers personal salvation as its service, and thereby abnegates the institutional changes that could indeed help the men.

Missions

It seems doubtful that the Skid Row missions can be abstracted into a convenient typology without discarding all but a few of their more superficial qualities. A yardstick of description is drafted here in favor of the intuitive typologies presented by other researchers (see table 2.2).

TABLE 2.2 MISSION SIZES AND SERVICES (Chicago, 1974)

Mission Name	Men Serviced*	Food	Shelter	Number of Men on Mission Program	Other Services	Legally Responsible for Mission	Source of Funds
Calvary Army (1956)	5-30	5-30		7-14	Store	Swift	Store with Donated Items
Pentacostal (1966)	150-200	150-200		2-5		Coleman	Speaking to Congregations
Bible Rescue (1957)	300	300		20-30	Factory	Board of Directors (15)	Speaking to Congregations, Factory, Mail Contributions
Holy Cross** (1916)	270	250		31	Clothing, Job Referral	Catholic Charities	Catholic Charities, Mail Contributions
West Side Rescue (1930?)	150	150		5		Board of Directors	Speaking to Congregations
Salvation Army (1922)	620	400	400	60	Clothing, Medical Psychiatric, Store, Factory Halfway House	Advisory Board	Salvation Army Stores, Government, Mail Contributions, Factories
Chicago United (1901)	125-150	125-150		6		Board of Directors	Speaking to Congregations
Pacific Garden (1880)	500	350	150	X	Medical Services	Board of Directors (16)	Mail Contributions from all over the world

TABLE 2.2 MISSION SIZES AND SERVICES (Chicago, 1974)

Mission Name	Men Serviced*	Food	Shelter	Number of Men on Mission Program	Other Services	Legally Responsible for Mission	Source of Funds
Helping Hand (1913)	150	X	X	X	Clothing	Christian Reform Church	Christian Reform Church
Olive Branch (1876)	100-140	60-90		3-5	Clothing	Board of Directors	Speaking to Congregations
Chicago Gospel (1882)	50-80	50-80	1-4 Bed Tickets	4-12	Clothing	Board of Directors	Free Methodist Churches, Foundation
Cathedral Shelter** (1919)	30-35	30-35	20-25	X	Clothing	Episcopal Church Board of Trustees	Episcopal Church Government
Chicago Christian Industrial League (1909)	1,000	600-800	290	130	Clothing, Store, Factory, Medical, Halfway House	Board of Directors (19)	Presbyterian Church

*Men per day.
**Note that the Catholic and Episcopal missions do *not* have the compulsory services and evangelical orientation.
X Program exists; no figures given by directors.

The mission staff usually consists of a director and his assistants, all of whom have received the "divine calling." Most of the missions are a part of a larger hierarchy and are technically regulated by church related policy making boards. As such, the missions are patrimonial bureaucracies using rational methods and universalistic criteria to attain goals of questionable rationality (although not questionable to the directors).

When we examine the internal structure of the missions, however, the relationship between articulated goals of the missions and the matter of fact world of Skid Row shows a marked disjuncture. The missions provide a variety of services for the men: food, clothing, shelter, the "true" Gospel, and various opportunities for "rehabilitation" through work in the missions or in mission related business activities.

The majority of missions see their primary goal as "reaching the men for Christ"; in fact the only ones concerned with providing certain necessities without the luxuries of Jesus are the Episcopal and Catholic sponsored organizations. All Skid Row missions give

A soup line

24

out food. This provision is used as the major incentive for attendance at the fundamentalist religious services.

Every day Skid Row "bums" will stand in a soup line waiting for a
preacher to shout his Billy Sunday-fanatic brand of Christianity.
The men thus assure themselves of a "supper" which normally
consists of a bowl of soup and one or two dried up rolls or pieces of
bread. In a few instances, old sandwiches are issued to the Skid
Row fold. Therefore, the missions are filled with bored, tired, unin-
terested men undergoing one to two hours of fire, brimstone, dam-
nation, approbation, and salvation. The Skid Row term for this
sermon is "earbeating," an incisive term which summarizes the
men's attitudes toward the ordeal.

The following is one example:

Without the Lord we can do nothing! After all is said and done, ya
can't expect mortals ta live free from sin, until sin is eradicated. Jesus
came all the way from the ivory palaces of heaven for one specific
purpose, and that is ta bring into existence a plan of salvation that
would absolutely positively get rid of sin. So now if somethin' tells you,
an' somethin' tells me that ya can't live without sin, until ya get rid of sin
in the first place. Doesn't that sound logical? Say amen.

One of the greatest mysteries in the world today is somethin' that I'd
like ta talk about tonight. This is the mystery of Godliness. In the book
First Timothy, Three Sixteen, it goes like this: Paul stated, 'Great is the
mystery of Godliness. God was manifest in the flesh, justified in the
spirit, believed on in the world, seen of angels, received up into glory.'
Now the emphasis on that scripture is: great is the mystery of Godliness, meaning that how can it be possible for a mortal that's living in a
world that's so embedded, an' enthrilled, an' infilled with the sin, how
can an individual live a Godly life? Well it's a mystery. But its being
done. I want you birds ta look up here, an' look at me right in the eye.
Ya might never of seen a guy before that lived free from sin. Yes,
you're lookin' into the face of a converted sinner. But nevertheless I
want ya ta know that I know what I'm doin', an' if I didn't think that I was
livin' free from sin, I wouldn't be up here tryin' ta tell ya that ya could do
it. So it's mysterious how that I can walk up State Street, walk up any
street of any city, whether it may be skid row, or any place in any town.
It is a mystery how that a person can walk up an' down the streets in
such of a rotten city like Chicago—sex immorals, sex perverts, sex
shows, sex books, sex stores, an' everything that's rotten. Come on,
say amen! It's a mystery how that a man can do it. But I'm here ta tell ya
how it can be done.

After all is said and done, you an' I are puny mortals that have got ta

25

A mission service

After the religious service, men are given food.

come ta God's conditions and God's demands. After all is said an' done, you an' I have ta agree with the fact that God is good. Come on, say amen! He's so good that he thought of you right down here on Madison Street. Right now the Lord looked down the telescope of time an' he saw that you an' I were helpless; that we could not help ourselves. Come on, say amen!

Fellas, I want ta tell ya somethin'. The Bible tells us that Jesus came into the world ta seek. Do ya think you an' I are worthy of the Lord Jesus Christ seekin' us? No, no, a thousand times no! But he thought so much of the poor that he came all the way from the ivory palaces of heaven in the form of a man out ta seek ta save that which was lost. He knew that we couldn't help ourselves, an' in so doin' whenever he went into the city of Nazareth, into the synagogue, they gave him the book an' he opened it an' read. What did he read? He said these words in the presence of all those chief priests, an' all of the high collars an' all of the sophisticated religious men of the day. He said these words as Isaiah prophetized. He said, 'The spirit of the Lord is upon me because,' let's all say because. The reason why the spirit of the Lord is on Jesus, he said, 'The spirit of the Lord is upon me because he has annointed me ta preach the gospel ta the poor and deliver the captives, set them that are bound free an' set those that are in prison free,' an' until Jesus came along ta me, I was bound down by the shackles of sin. I'm tellin' on myself. I know it was wrong ta smoke; I'd throw away my cigarettes time after time, an' you'd be surprised how many drank their last bottle an' said they was never goin' to drink again, but did ya know what? It doesn't take very long for that leaf ta turn right back again, because it's not within man ta direct his own footsteps. It's not within man ta live free from sin. Ya just can't do it. But Jesus came ta bring into existence a plan of salvation. That's the remedy that has ta be paid. That's the price is ta get your name written in the book of heaven by being saved. An' of all things, if there's anybody under the sun that ought ta know what salvation is, a God-called preacher should. Say amen!

Jesus told the disciples these words, that 'when I'm gone away, I'm goin' ta send the Holy Spirit. An' when ya get the Holy Ghost it will give ya power.' Not weakness—POWER! Power to say yes ta God an' no ta the devil. When ya get the baptism of the Holy Ghost they can take old Jim Beam an' throw it all over ya an' still it won't effect ya. That ol' Schlitz that made Milwaukee famous will cause ya ta think, 'Oh God save Chicago!' Come on, say amen!

Ya know what Jesus said? I want ta tell ya what the real Savior said. He gathered them ol' high priests around him an' he said, 'Come here. I got somethin' ta tell you gentlemen. Ya look like Christians, but on the inside you're full o' rottenness an' dead man's bones.' He said, 'I got a story ta tell ya.' He said, 'The harlots an' the whoremongers an' the sinners will go inta heaven before ya.' And' so what are we goin' ta see

27

in heaven? We're gonna see alot of converted sinners that admit they were sinners an' come ta Jesus just like they are. One time there was a meetin' at one of our churches an' as they were singin', there was an ol' harlot went past. There she was in ol' tattered clothing; she was just an ol' wreck. Nobody cared for her. Her life was spent in riotous livin'. She laid practically with every man there was around the countryside. Nobody thought anything of her; she was just an old harlot. But when she went by, she heard the songs of Zion, an' she felt somethin' git ahold of her. She turned around an' went back an' looked in the door of that little ol' humble church where she saw the Christian ladies with their dresses down where they belong, an' with their hair like it should be, long, an' how they look without lipstick an' rouge an' all that. An' when she looked over that congregation she saw a group of people that looked different. An' that night whenever they began ta give the altar call, she stood at the door an' she listened. An' did ya know the great God of heaven—that's why I love Jesus, because he loves the vilest of sinners, I don't care who they are. Ya know fellas, if ya want ta be a Christian, ya want to be a real one or none at all. Git out there an' live it up an' go ta hell like a man should. Let me tell ya somethin'. We got one nation called Russia an' Communist China. Russia does not believe in God. Like an ol' tough sinner, 'I don't believe in God' they say. Why, uh, uh, the cosmonauts went up around the earth, up in the heavens an' they came back. They said. 'We was up there all in heaven, we looked all around an' we couldn't find God no place.' So this little ol' harlot looked into the back of the church, nobody cared anything at all of her, but when she came in there she made her way up ta that altar. She bowed there in that little ol' bundle o' rags, she raised her hands towards heaven an' she said these words: 'Take me God just as I am. Oh God I got nothin' ta offer ya, but take me just as I am.' I want ya ta know fellas that God of heaven, the sinful condition of you an' I, or I was in an' you are in, presents a challange ta God. That God can reach all the way from the portals of heaven right down inta the muck an' the mire of sin, an' he won't let ya in there an' kinda slide a little bit off it at times. He'll pull ya right out. Repent! There's the mystery of salvation! Come on, say amen!

Now look up here you guys! Now I want ya ta listen ta me! Look up here! Look up here you guys! If ya go ta hell, it's not because this Bible is not plain ta understand. You can read it! Thank God, hallelujah! Let's all say hallelujah! Say it louder, hallelujah! Did ya know that name hallelujah is the same in the Chinese language, Japanese language, an' the Italian language, the German language, an' the Polocks even have to say it too if they want ta glorify God. Hallelujah; it's the same in all languages. Look up here fellas. Now look at me! In case ya don't know it, ya know I'm not just up here blowin' my bugle ta hear my head roar! When Jesus comes I'm plannin' on leavin' this little ol' planet called earth, an' you're a fool if ya stay here when he comes. Cause brother whenever he comes ta take us out o' this world, then the wrath of God is gonna be revealed against a Christ rejectin' generation.

Everybody's wrong but the Bible. Let me tell ya somethin'. Look up here! I used ta go ta everything whether it was sports an' sin, an' entertainment. I have not been ta theatre in over thirty some years. I want ya ta know ya may think I'm a dipilapidated fool, but I wanna tell ya somethin'. I haven't read a comic paper in over thirty some years. They don't make comic papers for Christians; they make them for sinners. They're ungodly stuff today! Come on, say amen!

Don't ever tell me ya can't live a Christian life in this rotten world. I'll stand there at the judgment bar as a testimony against ya, that it could be done an' was done! Everyone say amen! You'll never be able ta quit the bottle within yourself. I know a tramp eight ta ten years ago. He went back home, an' they came back ta skid row, an' when they come back here they don't come back ta drink Pepsi-Cola. They come back ta git acquainted with ol' white port. Listen ta me! You can do it. You can live right. Look up here you guys! You can git in this great battle against the devil. The Bible says that we should be but the soldiers of Jesus Christ, an' that we should fight the good fight of faith an' the devil hasn't got a chance. Now look up here! Time is rollin' on; ten years, fifteen years, twenty-five years—twenty-five years from now the biggest portion of ya won't be alive. Well listen you guys. Let me say this: please, please think. You're gonna die someday; think! Don't be a fool and die without God, when Jesus Christ paid the price that set you an' I right. Take advantage of it! Remember, taking Jesus into your life is like a circumcision of the heart. How many want ta go ta heaven please raise your hand. . . .

At the end of the sermon, the men eat, and that is why they came.

Germane to this discussion is an adopted policy which is standard among all Skid Row missions whereby one who is intoxicated is denied access to or thrown out of a mission. Many times, those most in need of help are rejected.

The Programs

In addition to offering food, the missions frequently provide donated clothes and a few provide lodging. A couple of the missions give limited medical care and psychiatric help, but in most missions one of the major services is the program.

All missions incorporate into their catalogue of services what is known as an "alcoholic program." Men off the street, in a fit of desperation, submit to joining such a program. However, before a man is accepted on a mission program, he must "take a nose dive" (go to the altar during a service and profess conversion).

It deserves attention that blacks and, in many cases, Indians are excluded from these mission playgrounds. The mission directors assert with no indecision that only certain racial stocks are designated by God for salvation.

After "getting saved," the reformed individual is assigned menial tasks such as janitorial or food preparation activities, or in some missions employed in a church operated business, in exchange for living accommodations and board at the missions. Daily attendance at services with subsequent testimonials like, "I used to be a sinner, but now that I've taken Jesus into my heart . . . ," and Bible reading sessions are compulsory. Men on the programs are treated like children incapable of thinking for themselves. They are extended a nominal allowance of $2.00 to $5.00 per week. All overt expressions of speech and movement are suppressed in favor of a tacit mindlessness which pontificates those specific verses of the New Testament which distinguish the much emphasized theological viewpoints of whatever mission they have taken residence. The mission programs encounter high attrition rates. In most of the missions, only half of one percent are "rehabilitated" after one year.[2] The average man tolerates a program for one to three months. When one takes leave of a program, another is admitted in his place. The missions continually exploit this inexhaustable supply of cheap labor.

The missions remain undaunted in the face of their blatant failure to rehabilitate the men. Their self-evaluations are impervious to reality. Like other bureaucracies they keep diligent records of meals, clothes, shelter, conversions, and participants on the programs as measures of their success. The fact that some men have been "saved" hundreds of times is not considered. "Success" is evaluated by the goods and services and *not* by "rehabilitation" rates.

Moreover, the structural characteristics of the individual Skid Row missions undermine and inhibit any consequential progress within that social framework. Edward Spicer (1970) has described certain types of patron-client relationships as disruptive. In order for the client to receive the needed goods and services, he must demonstrate a value orientation similar to that of the patrons. The paternalistic mission program has implicit problems for the Skid Row clientele in that it severs their primary group relationships. To be "rehabilitated," the Skid Rower must abandon his consorts, abdicate his lifestyle and identity, and accomodate himself in the sterile ideologies of a mission program.

This introduces a state of conflict which exists between the "tramp" and the program men (mission stiffs). The Skid Row term "mission stiff" anticipates these sentiments. In its widest understanding, "mission stiff" refers to either a man on a mission program, or the individual who frequents the mission services on a daily basis. Invariably, it suggests demeaning connotations.

Another common feature of the Skid Row mission is its compulsive adherence to schedules. These missions operate unremittingly within this rigid scheduling usually independent of urgency of need. A man must be at the mission at the designated time or else he is denied whatever assistance he is seeking. For example, after a mission service begins, the doors are promptly locked. A "down and out" man who is late is thus without food and/or lodging for the night. Rarely is a latecomer admitted.

A telling example of this intransigence occurred one evening during a torrential cloud burst. Twenty-five men were waiting in a soup line in front of a mission. They were soon inundated with rain as they stood outside while unconcerned mission employees observed them. It seemed quite implausible to the mission director and his staff that the men outside might dislike getting wet and cold, and under the circumstances would have preferred not waiting outside for the five minutes till the mission "officially" opened.

Those missions offering nightly shelter shove the men out in the morning at the assigned time (5:00 A.M., 5:30 A.M., 6:00 A.M.) regardless of whether or not they have another place to go, or what the weather conditions are.

Income

Skid Row missions seize a variety of means in securing their "daily bread." The missions are generally known as poverty-strick-

31

en agencies begging for contributions. In fact, they are well financed. Most of the operating funds come from traditional sources, such as individual benefactors, foundations or contributions from specific denominations or congregations where missionaries make appearances requesting support for Christ's work on Skid Row. In their appeal for money, they cite the aforementioned records of their accomplishments for Christ. At least two of the missions receive funds from the government. A rather unusual, though significant, means of income is found in the men of Skid Row. When a Skid Row mission accepts a man in its "alcoholic program," a routine attempt is made to get this person on welfare or another form of assistance, in which event, the mission staff assumes responsibility vis a vis proprietorship of all or large portions of his checks.

A second method by which Skid Row men assist in financing these religious firms is by working in the stores and factories managed by a number of the missions. In these enterprises of the Skid Row missions, program men are expected to comply with "work therapy" as a necessary component for "rehabilitation." The men work an eight hour day for five or six days per week, in different capacities of the operation, namely the collecting, repairing, and reselling of donated items. Salaries range from $2.00 to $12.00 per week, scaled proportionately to seniority and indispensability of position. Again, the turnover is exceedingly high. Profits from these stores not only make the missions self-sustaining, but may also be utilized for missionary work in other areas.

Expenses

Mission expenses are minimal. There are two reasons for this. First, missions are for the most part exempt from taxes by virtue of their non-profit charter. Second, all food dispensed by the missions is donated by large companies. An underlying consideration of these industrial philanthropists is that "contributions" are deductible for tax purposes. It is more profitable to give away stale or surplus food than to have it destroyed. These generally dated and/or anutritional food substitutes satisfy the men's immediate physical hunger, and ensure a congregation for the mission.

Conclusion and Summary

The missions' attempts to provide amelioration of institutional dysfunctions through religious palliatives not only fails, but in fact, the missions who offer "salvation" in many ways contribute to the existence of Skid Row. The ineptitude of the mission caretakers is considerable by all those professional standards to which they assume to address themselves. This is most notable in their alcoholic programs which incur infinitesimal rates of success. Perhaps the real tragedy here is that the religious intercession in this subculture obfuscates rather than effectively deals with the men's problems or needs. The Skid Row missions routinely and systematically maintain their institutions independent of all but the most subsistent needs of the Skid Row men.

Skid Row missionaries, whose *raison d'être* is couched in evangelical fundamentalism, who lack qualifications and expertise, prove incapable of understanding Skid Row beyond the simple-minded diagnosis, sin, and the offering of the prescription to embrace Christ. Perhaps the most significant consequence of the missionaries' efforts for "salvation" on Skid Row is their own attainment of income, status, and power.

The existence of the missions is used as justification for political and social indifference which explains failure in the economic system as due solely to the innate character deficiencies of the "unsuccessful."

Notes

[1]Members of ethnic groups (American Indians, Blacks, Mexican Americans, Puerto-Ricans, Southern Whites) which occupy the lowest economic position in the United States are far more likely to end up on Skid Row than persons of other backgrounds.

[2]In a couple of the smaller missions there are instances when a man from Skid Row has remained with a mission for a number of years.

Chapter III

Hotels

Skid Row hotels are a major institution determining the existence of this urban culture. These $1.35 to $3.00 a night hotels, catering to the economically displaced, give a common locality to such individuals.

In 1909, there were two types of cheap (10¢ to 25¢ a night) lodging houses in Chicago for "unattached" working men: the dormitory (the more common and popular with the men at this time), and the small room (cubicle). Before these were built in the late 1880's and early 1890's, "homeless" men roomed in private houses or cheap hotels near their place of work (Solenberger, 1909). Thirty-one years later, Nels Anderson described lodging houses or flophouses on Chicago's hobohemia "where for a nickle or a dime one can sleep on the floor, where for twenty-five cents one can sleep on a cot in a dormitory and have blankets, or where for thirty-five cents or a half a dollar one can sleep in a cubicle" (Anderson, 1940:13).

A reduction in the number of cubicle hotels in the last fifty years has resulted from a decline in the Skid Row population, a rise in expenses, restrictions imposed by building ordinances, and in recent years Urban Renewal projects.

In 1923, a survey of lodging house and hotel populations indicated that there were 25,000 to 30,000 "homeless men" in Chicago (Anderson, 1923:14). An estimate of the number of "homeless men" in Chicago's Skid Rows in 1957, based upon hotel and rooming houses in the West Madison and South State areas,

35

placed the Skid Row population at 11,926. On West Madison alone there were twenty-one cubicle hotels housing over six thousand men (Newman, 1961). At the time my research was initiated, 1970, there were approximately 8,000 men on Chicago's Skid Rows. In the West Madison Skid Row area there were fourteen cubicle hotels. In 1974 there were eight. Presently there are only three.

Rising expenses (insurance, electricity, coal, linen, etc.), along with building and health codes have forced the more deteriorated hotels out of business and discouraged construction of cubicle hotels.

Chapter 78.1 of the Municipal Codes of Chicago lists building specifications for existing[1] men's cubicle hotels. These are com-

TABLE 3.1 BUILDING CODES FOR
CUBICLE HOTELS AND OTHER STRUCTURES

	Men's Cubicle Hotels	Other Buildings and Hotels
SPATIAL REQUIRE – MENTS	The number of occupants permitted on a floor is computed by taking the total square feet from wall to wall of a floor and dividing the number by 50. (Each cubicle is 7' x 5' or 35 square feet. Hallways, stairways and washrooms make up the difference.	70 square feet per room per person.
SANITARY FACILITIES	At least one flush water closet, lavatory basin and bath tub, or shower, for each twenty persons.	At least one flush water closet, basin and bath for each ten persons.
VENTILATION	No requirements.	5% of floor area.
FIRE EXTINGUISHER APPARATUS	After 1956, every existing or pre-ordinance multiple dwelling building must have a sprinkler system and be separated by walls which are fire resistant for not less than one hour.	

36

pared in Table 3.1 with those specifications for other buildings and hotels.

If it were not for the modifications of normal building ordinances, men's cubicle hotels would be forced to close. Even so, no Skid Row cubicle hotels have been built in recent decades. This is due specifically to natural lighting laws. (Pre-ordinance hotels are not affected by natural lighting laws). These laws basically hold that all residential units (rooms) must have some means of effectively transmitting light from the outside. The area of glass in a room cannot be less than 10% of the floor area.

Before a building or structure may be constructed, altered, or demolished, a permit must be obtained from the commissioner of buildings. To receive this certificate, a floor plan of the building must be given to the building commissioner. The commissioner then decides whether the plans conform to applicable building codes or not. As a result, with the natural lighting ordinance, it is not against the law to build men's cubicle hotels, it simply becomes economically impractical.

On the basis of physical characteristics Skid Row hotels can be classified into two types: 1) cubicle, and 2) room. A room in a cubicle hotel is usually 7 feet in length, 5 feet in width, and 7 1/2 feet in height. All rooms have a door with a lock and are partitioned by plaster board or corrugated metal walls. Each cubicle has a steel bed frame 6 feet by 3 feet. Upon this is an old mattress 3 inches thick (often replete with bed bugs), one dusty blanket (rarely if ever washed), sheets, pillow and case (the filth of which often defies adjectives). These rooms also have stools and metal lockers (16 inches in width and depth, 7 feet in height) for clothes. Men bolt themselves in their rooms while they sleep, and hang their clothes (with money) inside lockers as precautionary strategems against theft. Rooms have no electrical outlets; a 25 watt bulb suspended from chicken wire is the only source of light. Few rooms in cubicle hotels have access to a window. Thus, to maximize on deficient ventilation, cubicles have only wire mesh ceilings (to impede unlawful visitors), and a four inch gap between floor and walls. Air fetid from stale wine, vomit and urine, cockroaches, lice, and sometimes rats, are facts of the flophouses. To prevent themselves from

TABLE 3.2
CUBICLE HOTEL WASHROOM FACILITIES*

Cubicle Hotels	No. of Rooms Per Floor	No. of Toilets** Per Floor	Avg. No. of Men For Ea. Toilet	No. of Showers Per Floor	Avg. No. of Men For Ea. Shower	No. of Baths Per Floor	Avg. No. of Men Per Bath
Chicago Mills	238	8	29	3	79	1	238
Golden Arcade	73	3	24	1	24	0	—
Ideal	110	4	28	1	110	1	110
Lindy	80	4	20	2	40	0	—
Legion	169	7	24	7	24	1	169
McCoy	280	12	23	4	45	2	140
Mohawk	185	10	18	7	25	1	185
Starr	97	3	32	2	48	1	97
Working Man's Palace	111	4	27	4	27	0	—

*Toilets, showers and baths not in working order are included in these figures.
**Urinals not considered.

A room in a cubicle hotel

getting lousy, some men lodging in these hotels will keep in their possession a can of insecticide. The never ending coughing, snoring, moaning, shouting, and arguing in many cubicle hotels is audible to anyone on a floor. Toilets and washing facilities in cubicle hotels are overcrowded and often in need of repair.

Minimal cost per night in cubicle hotels is $1.35 to $2.00. Room hotels are more quiet and, unlike many flophouses, do not suffer from an indifference to disorder. The minimum charge of these hotels is from $2.50 to $3.50 per night. All Skid Row hotels have reduced weekly or monthly rates.

Only four hotels on Madison Street Skid Row accept women. These women meet their living expenses by 1) being recipients of public aid, 2) sharing accomodations with men, or 3) prostituting themselves.

Nothing seems to offend the sensibilities of those unfamiliar with Skid Row life more than its uncleanliness. For a century, researchers and casual observers alike have been appalled by the substandard conditions in Skid Row flophouses. The graphic details have become a tradition particularly with the cursory writer on the subject. Unmindful of all but sensationalism, many fail to understand that Skid Rowers voluntarily live in such conditions. If money were no restriction, most men living in Skid Row hotels would seek accomodations in more fashionable surroundings. Life on Skid Row becomes a choice among severely limited alternatives (such as geriatric wards, alcoholic programs, jail, a cheap apartment room and/or a low paying job in another community).

Skid Row hotels offer unique services for their customers which they would receive nowhere else. Companionship, low cost, protection and care, and autonomy are the principal factors which govern a man's decision to live in a Skid Row hotel.

In lobbies of Skid Row hotels, men are always present, most only for a few hours a day. Here they will pass the bottle, read newspapers, watch television, or play cards. In their rooms, men often talk and drink wine with acquaintances. Sometimes, if a man gets too drunk, is unable to work and has no money, a friend will lend him enough for food until he is able to work again. On a few occasions, hotel clerks will give a down and out man a room without charge.

Most Skid Row hotels pay close attention to their sick and elderly. If someone in the hotel is ill and confined to bed, the clerk sees to it that the man gets food or medicine. If the illness is serious, a clerk will notify an ambulance or the police that the man must be taken to a hospital. Men impaired by alcohol are assisted to their rooms by clerks and porters.

Hotels on Skid Row have safes in which lodgers may keep their money (usually monthly welfare or assistance checks). To eliminate loss of the entire sum through jackrolling, a man will only request at any one time small amounts of his money for which he is charged a service fee by the hotel.

Skid Row men, most of whom are without watches or alarm clocks, will ask the hotel clerk to awaken them at some hour in the morning to work day labor or a job. The clerk writes their room numbers and the time on a "call list." At that hour, their doors are pounded, usually until the men are out of bed.

Hotels for Skid Row men are by construction and regulations designed for security. To prevent jackrolling, men not registered are refused entrance beyond hotel lobbies. Offices of clerks are always positioned along entrances to turn away the non-paying element. In cubicle hotels, anytime a man leaves, he must turn over his room key to the clerk. After returning, he has to present a room receipt in order to get his key again. Almost all Skid Row hotels have these rules: 1) no visitors, 2) lobbies are closed from 10 P.M. to 5 A.M.

For the most part, Skid Row hotels do just what the men want—nothing. Those inclined to be reticent would have to drink themselves quite sick before hotel management would intervene. Nonetheless, unwritten laws are implicit in life at any hotel on Skid Row. Men who are quarrelsome or belligerent in a hotel become casualties to their justice. A bludgeon is kept by a number of clerks to substantiate their authority in these matters. The following example is one of many observed by the author.

In the Ideal Hotel lobby (on the afternoon of December 1, 1972), an American Indian went to the clerk to inquire about his financial standing in the hotel. After some words between the two men, the hotel clerk growled something about the man's money not covering his bill for the coming week. Emphatically the man contested,

A hotel lobby

"Wha'da ya mean? I paid!" The burly clerk's response was immediate and volatile. "Why you damn son of a bitch!" and he abruptly went after the man (now frightened and backing off) slamming him to the floor. As he went down his head cracked noticeably hard. He lay there dazed. The clerk dragged him out of the lobby, and promptly returned to his chores.

Over summer months, Skid Row hotels average forty to one hundred fewer men than their average winter number of clientele. In warm weather, many men sleep in old buildings, abandoned cars, alleys, parks, and so on, when heat and odors from lack of ventilation (particularly in cubicle hotels) become intolerable.

The population of sixteen Skid Row hotels is by rough estimate 67 percent white or 2,626 out of 3,858. Two hotels rent almost entirely to blacks while most other hotels do not accept these individuals. (See Table 3.3) Most men living in Skid Row hotels fall within the age bracket of thirty-five to sixty. Generally, about 60 to 75 percent of them receive pensions or some other form of financial assistance. Somewhere from ten to thirty percent of any hotel population work day labor a few days a week.

The fixed tendency of referring to the "homeless man" of Skid Row is standard in much of the sociological literature on the subject. Nevertheless, between five and twenty percent of the inhabitants of Skid Row hotels have lived in the same hotel for ten to forty years. The term seems to offer as much insight into the cognitive disposition of those social "scientists" as it does into the lives of Skid Row men.

The basic jobs of most Skid Row hotels are that of clerk, porter and maid. A clerk is the on-duty manager of the hotel. He tends the desk, writes in guests, takes in the daily money, calls police and maintains order within the hotel. Clerks work twelve hours a day, seven days a week. They are paid, varying with hotels, $8.00 to $12.00 a day, or 67¢ to $1.00 an hour (minimum wage is $1.60 an hour), plus a room in the hotel.

Porters clean up the hotel, take drunks to their rooms, and help keep order. A porter works twelve hours a day for seven days a week. Pay is four or five dollars a day. Also included is a room in the hotel. In actual work, they put in no more than two or three hours per

43

day. Clerks and porters without exception are recruited from Skid Row. Maids (black, female, between the ages of forty and sixty, and living on Chicago's South Side) change bed linen and clean rooms, a few hours a day, a couple days a week. Payment for their work is by the hour ($2.00 to $2.50). Further, maids make other favors available to the men in the hotels for about $5.00.

Although wages for clerks and porters are low and hours are long, work is not difficult. In addition, clerks and porters tend to be heavy drinkers and could not hold other types of steady employment. Not only is drinking on the job tolerated, but a man who is occasionally absent from work for a few days because of drunkenness will not lose his job.

Summary

The flophouses are a determining factor in the existence of Skid Row. The number of cubicle hotels on Skid Row has declined in recent years as a result of rising operating expenses, restrictions imposed by building ordinances, a general economic prosperity which has contributed to a reduction in the Skid Row population, and, most importantly, urban renewal.

The conditions in most of the Skid Row hotels today are deplorable. They are rarely cleaned and ventilation is poor. They stink of urine and vomit and are infested with rats and insects. The washrooms are unsanitary and the facilities are often in disrepair. Nevertheless, there are some advantages to living in flophouses, such as companionship, low cost, security and autonomy. In the hotels, men watch television, drink wine and talk with friends.

Notes

[1]By definition of Chicago Municipal Codes, an existing building is a building, structure or part thereof, which has been completed and is ready for occupancy after the effective date of this ordinance. A pre-ordinance building is every existing building, structure or part thereof, which was completed, or for the construction of which a permit was issued, prior to the effective date of this ordinance (Ammend. Coun. J. 1-20-50).

TABLE 3.3
HOTEL DATA

Hotel Name	Type	Minimum Cost Per Night	Average Occupancy of Rooms		Percent Receiving Some Type of Assist.
			Winter	Summer	
Burton House	Room	$1.50	500	400	X
Chicago Mills	Cubicle	$1.50	400	360	80
Collins	Room	$2.50	85	70	75
Golden Arcade	Cubicle	$1.50	140	120	65
Ideal	Cubicle	$1.50	230	225	X
Imperial	Room	$12.00 a week	70	60	85
Lindy	Cubicle	$1.40	175	140	70
Legion	Cubicle	$1.50	450	400	X
Major	Room	$2.50	145	100	X
McCoy	Cubicle	$1.35	500	400	X
Mohawk	Cubicle	$2.00	350	250	95
New Breslin	Room	$2.50	35	35	75
New Ogden	Room	$3.00	86	75	85
Starr	Cubicle	$1.35	300	250	50
Sylvian	Room	$3.00	62	35	95
Working Man's Palace	Cubicle	$1.50	330	270	83

X Information not given.

No interviews were taken at the New Albany, Standard, Pacific, and New Elite.

TABLE 3.3 — *Continued*

Hotel Name	Percent Who Work Day Labor	Nationality Percentages				Men's Age Percentages			Men Only
		Black	Indian	Span. speaking	White	Under 30	30-60	Over 60	
Burton House	X	96	*	*	4	X	X	X	
Chicago Mills	10	4	5	30	61	X	X	X	+
Collins	8	0	*	*	96	0	79	21	
Golden Arcade	15	0	4	*	96	0	75	25	+
Ideal	X	0	6	4	90	3	75	22	+
Imperial	15	0	*	70	30	0	80	20	+
Lindy	30	0	5	*	95	4	83	13	+
Legion	X	0	5	15	80	5	75	15	+
Major	X	0	0	0	100	0	65	35	+
McCoy	X	4	3	2	91	0	89	11	+
Mohawk	40	90	*	*	10	15	75	10	+
New Breslin	10	*	4	*	96	0	70	30	+
New Ogden	12	0	2	3	95	0	85	15	
Star	17	6	4	*	90	X	X	X	+
Sylvian	5	0	*	8	92	0	90	10	
Working Man's Palace	30	3	2	*	95	0	85	15	+

0 Never.

*Occasionally.

Chapter IV

Employment

Comic sections in newspapers occasionally depict Skid Row men with stubbly beards and patched clothing, sitting on park benches or walking down railroad tracks, carrying a bindle on a stick, as lazy ne'er-do-wells who would rather bum a dime than put in an honest day's work. Such gross exaggerations neglect the depressing realities of life on Skid Row.

Work on Skid Row is generally day labor. Labor agencies are essential to many Skid Row men who, without a steady job, are in need of money and find temporary work their only alternative. The wages are low, the work monotonous and/or hard. A man working out of these agencies earns just enough to survive from day to day. To save enough money to rise out Skid Row's poverty is for many a hopeless struggle. There is no job security for the day laborer. He is fired after each work day. If he is sick, he receives no compensation. The temporary employment offices are instrumental in the existence of Skid Row.

Types of Employment Agencies

In the West Madison Street Skid Row area, there are nineteen privately owned employment agencies, and two government operated agencies. The privately managed labor agencies can also be subgrouped into temporary contractors (of which there are sixteen[1]) and private employment agencies (of which there are three).

Temporary Contractors

Temporary contractors are the most important employment agencies for men on Skid Row, and Skid Row offers the "slave labor" offices rare opportunity for profit. Day labor agencies capitalize on the economically disadvantaged man of Skid Row, giving him the dirtiest and most undesirable of jobs, the worst hours, and the lowest pay.

In the early hours of a business day when downtown Chicago is, but for an occasional bus or taxi, nothing more than lonely sidewalks and buildings, Skid Row flourishes with life. Short-order restaurants are busy with men hurrying to eat breakfast before work. Men stand talking, waiting to get jobs at labor offices. Signs and windows of most day labor offices advertise "Daily Pay; Report For Work at 5:00 A.M." For many temporary workers, allowing for time to get ready, a day begins at four or four-thirty in the morning.

Day labor offices receive most of their job orders by mail or phone, usually the day before men are sent out to work. Only so many jobs are available. In the morning, as men enter an agency, they find a seat and wait until the management motions them individually to come to the office. Selected for a job, a man is merely asked his name and social security number. Some agencies describe the work before a man takes the job. All men are required to fill out Internal Revenue WW4 and State of Illinois forms the first time they apply for work at an agency.

A man who has a history at an agency of being a hard worker is given a job first. Men of "questionable reliability" (the elderly, those who have in the past walked off jobs, or those who have not worked to the expectations of a company) are the last to get a job. A man who has had no prior working experience at an agency has less trouble getting work. Good workers who are regulars with an agency are given jobs directly upon entrance. Other men[2] wait two to three hours for a job. Almost all jobs on order are given out by 7:00 A.M. Even so, ten to twenty-five men in each agency stay until 8:00 or 9:00 A.M., having only fatigued hind quarters for hours of waiting.

A major problem of the day labor offices is transporting workers to the jobs. A number of agencies provide a bus or a van. For this service there may be a charge of a dollar. Some agencies will drive a man to a factory for no charge, "giving" him a dollar or two to pay for his return. If a job is far away, agencies will give a man an advance and send him to work by public transit.[3] All advances are deducted from a man's earnings; as one Skid Row man remarked, "Them day labor offices got a hand in your pocket to start with."

All employees of day labor take a written authorization to the job. This "voucher" includes the name and address of the labor office and the contracting business, and the hour a man is to start work. It usually must be presented to the work supervisor who retains it either until the workday is completed or a man elects to quit. In either event, the supervisor records the number of hours worked and signs his name on the bottom of the voucher. If a day labor worker "walks off" the job, companies are required to pay the agency only for the number of hours he worked. Otherwise, companies must pay day labor offices a minimum of four hours per man.

Once the job is completed, the expendable day laborer is retired from the company. The worker must then return to the labor agency with the voucher indicating the number of hours he has worked. If the agency is still open (most day labor offices close in the early afternoon), a man is given his check there. Payment is made according to the hours worked.[4] The agency then instructs the man where he may cash the check, usually a tavern or restaurant. If the labor office is not open, the man must pick up his check and cash it at a specified tavern. Working day labor—from the time a man enters the labor office until he is paid—thus involves ten to twelve hours of a man's day.

For the average Skid Row man working day labor, total earnings for eight hours of work are $12.80, or $1.60 per hour.[5] After deductions of 80¢ for social security and $1 to $2 for transportation, net pay is about $10 or $11 per work day. Companies pay day labor offices $2.45 to $2.75 per hour for this same man. Many day labor offices do not pay a man overtime until he has worked over forty hours a week for the same company. Most day labor offices bill their clients by the week to absorb the daily expense of workers' wages.

As recently as two years ago, companies interested in hiring a day labor worker were threatened with fines under a penalty clause. Today day labor offices cannot legally restrain one of their men from taking a permanent job at a company. Consequently,

49

labor agencies use much persuasive art to discourage companies from hiring their workers: "These men don't want a steady job. They'll quit after a week, a month at the longest. You'll only regret it."

Types of Day Labor Jobs

Employees of day labor offices are fully insured, and there are no restrictions other than handling money and driving motor vehicles. Jobs given day labor workers by most businesses demand no skills, and are usually too boring and/or too dirty for permanent employees. Most such jobs are 1) general labor in factories, 2) loading and unloading trucks, and 3) trade show work.

To many companies a man working day labor is an expendable object intended only to promote financial gain. This is illustrated by the following example. Every day a labor office on Madison Street sent five men from Skid Row to work at a factory which manufactures chemical insecticides. Before starting to work, day laborers put on overalls, rubber gloves and gas masks (masks were found to have parts missing and were also contaminated with a toxic chemical). In the job, men were required to fill trays 12'' by 16'' with a pesticide powder which was heaped on a large table. Trays were then placed in a holder to be heated. The job was unbearable; most men "walked off" after an hour or two. Getting sick to their stomachs and passing out were routine occurrences for these workers. Unsuspecting men, needing money, are sent each day to work at this company.

Trucks and boxcars, if detained by a company beyond the time allowed for loading or unloading, must pay a demurrage charge. Spot labor is a practical answer to a company confronted with this situation. The work is usually exhausting and requires much physical endurance. A man on Skid Row talked about a recent job at a printing factory where he had to unload 125 lb. packages from a boxcar. "It was too much for me! After three hours I didn't ask for anything; I just plain walked off and quit. I swore I'd be hungry before I went back there."

Trade shows at McCormick Place and the Amphitheatre use day

labor offices for temporary help. Skid Row men push crates from loading docks to the locations where the displays are assembled, or sweep up after shows.

Why Companies Use Day Labor

Day labor offices exist to the economic advantage of many companies. When additional help is needed, it is certainly more convenient to call a labor agency than to have a company employee coax someone off the street to work for a day. Using day labor workers, companies do not pay insurance or hospitalization benefits. The entire sum paid to a day labor office can be claimed as a tax exemption by a company. Moreover, a company using day labor help has considerably less bookkeeping work, since it does not have to keep records of social security and federal and state income tax, etc. for each of its employees.

Private Employment Agencies

Private employment bureaus differ from the temporary or day labor agencies most importantly in that the former refer a job applicant to a business which takes on the worker as its employee, whereas day labor offices send men out to companies as their own employees.

Applicants from these agencies are usually sent to work in restaurants, less often to country clubs or camps. The jobs may be short term (80% last a day or so), or permanent. Jobs such as dishwasher, porter, cook, and waiter are usually the only positions available in the three private employment agencies on Skid Row. These jobs are also among the lowest paying employment in the country. A dishwasher or porter normally earns $15.00 per ten hour day (nine hours of work plus a free meal). A man working out of a private employment agency on Skid Row on a daily basis usually earns no more than $1.30 an hour, after paying the agency's fees.

A Skid Row man looking for a job may go to one of these agencies at almost any hour of the day, seven days a week.

However, the individual interested in casual employment will have less difficulty securing a job if he reports to an agency early in the morning. The applicant must pay a placement fee to the agency, which varies with the type and duration of job. For a temporary job as a cook or waiter, the fee is $2.50; for porters and dishwashers, $2.00. Steady job fees for employment as a cook or waiter are $30.00, as a dishwasher or porter, $20.00. If a man does not get the job, the agency must refund the fee, unless he 1) is late for work, 2) reports to work under the influence of alcohol, 3) walks off the job, or 4) doesn't give the employer a satisfactory day's work.

By law these agencies are required to keep records showing the date an order is received, the name and address of the employer placing the order, the job offered, the wages paid, the name of the applicant, duration of job, the day he is sent out, and the amount of the placement fee.

Every man who is sent out for a job is given a "referral slip" which lists the name of the applicant, the name and address of the agency and the employer, the type of job, hours of work, and/or wages.

The Department of Labor has authority to grant or revoke the license of a private employment agency. Without such a license these agencies cannot conduct business in the state of Illinois. If any agency does not comply with the provisions of any of these laws, it can be put out of business. Agency records are subject to inspection by department officials.

Public Day Labor Offices

Madison Street Skid Row has two Illinois State Employment Offices offering day labor work. These agencies act only in referring jobs. Men who work out of these public agencies make $2.00 to $2.50 an hour for the same jobs for which private agencies pay $1.60 an hour. Public day labor offices by law may not discriminate, and therefore must accept every applicant. Unlike private agencies, they cannot "blackball" a man who is not a "capable" worker. Many companies thus prefer private agencies because they get more "controlled help." The law also specifies that veterans (particularly handicapped veterans) must be given first consideration for a job. Before a man takes a job at a government agency, he is told how much the job pays and the type of work demanded of him.

The public agencies keep information on their applicants. Records include a man's name, his address, social security number, driver's license (if a man has one), and visible handicaps. Also, older men are asked if they have a "health condition", so that a man will not be sent on a job where there is an apparent risk of getting hurt.

Other Labor

Bottle Collecting Agency

Cheap wine is an obvious part of Skid Row life. On the street, in hotel lobbies, almost anywhere, men share bottles. After the wine is guzzled, the bottle is usually tossed away. One might expect some accumulation of these bottles in vacant lots and alleys over a length of time, save for one fact. A business on Sangamon and Madison pays old men to scavenge through the alleys, street gutters, and trash containers of Skid Row to find used wine bottles. A bottle collector carefully examines each bottle for any remaining gulps of wine. They are paid $1/2$¢ for each bottle.

Delivering Handbills

Sprague is a business on Madison which distributes advertisements for other companies door to door in Chicago and suburban neighborhoods. If a man intends to peddle bills for Sprague, he must be at the office no later than 5:30 A.M. Men are selected for work by the drivers of five to ten trucks. After the men are chosen, they cart and load advertising material on the trucks. Canvas bags with shoulder straps, a bag of rubber bands, and a stack of 1,000 handbills are given to the eight to twelve workers in each truck. Each man is then assigned to cover an area. The driver supervises the men by occasional appearances in the different areas. Any man who is caught "dumping" his bills forfeits his ten dollars pay. On the day a man works, he gets a check for six dollars; he must return one day the following week to collect the remaining portion of his check. Out of this money, 50¢ goes to a Distributors Union. Many men who

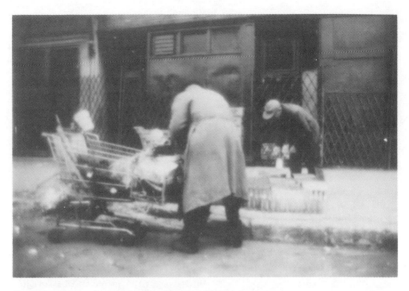

Before men are paid by the Bottle Collection Agency they must place their empty wine bottles in boxes.

Needing work, Skid Row men wait for trucks on the corner of DesPlains and Monroe.

work for Sprague complain that drivers ask them for two or three dollars. As one worker put it, "It's simple. If you don't pay, you don't go out."

Peterson Barrel Company

Peterson Barrel Company on Monroe and Green Streets pays 25¢ for every cardboard barrel, three feet in height with a steel rim, brought to them. Men are given 25¢ for two "dumbies": barrels without rims. Skid Row men get these barrels from the garbage of the meat and fish packing companies in the Fulton Market area just north of Madison Street. A man can carry up to four barrels at a time by making a small hole at the top of each, tying them together with rope and hanging them over his shoulders.

Other Non-Agency Jobs

Many jobs available to men on Skid Row are not acquired through labor agencies. Throughout most of the day, a half dozen to twenty men gather on the corners of DesPlaines and Monroe, and Jefferson and Monroe to wait for trucks such as moving vans which offer individuals a job for the day. This work pays somewhat better than employment agencies. However a man can wait two or three hours on a corner and not get work.

Also, many factories and other businesses in the area surrounding Madison Street take on men from Skid Row to work odd jobs without the "benefits" of an employment agency. Such men are known as "walk-ins."

During the summer and early fall, trucks from Illinois, Indiana, Michigan, and Wisconsin head for Madison Skid Row to entice men to work on farms picking fruits and vegetables. To men on Skid Row whose minds are sufficiently dulled by alcohol, the work is made to seem like a vacation at a health spa. "You want three meals a day, a clean bed, fresh air, money? Get in the truck." Unfortunately the jobs leave many men angered and disgusted. A man remembers an experience he had a few years ago:

55

I went picking tomatoes down in Indiana last year. You'll never get me down there again. I was over at the Salvation Army one Sunday morning. This guy had his truck parked out in front. He come out there and said, 'You want to go to Indiana and pick some tomatoes?' I said, 'Yeah,' cause he had a pint of wine in his truck. 'Yeah, I'll go to Indiana and pick some tomatoes.' They get you down there—they had an old five room house, no electricity, no inside toilet. You go in and sleep on the floor—they got mattresses throwed over the floor. They bring around the wine and sell it to you a dollar a pint. You pick tomatoes to pay it off. They pay you twenty-five cents for a bushel of tomatoes you pick. They charge you seven dollars a day for room and board. They give you food like oatmeal or baloney sandwiches. After six days, I wound up owing them money. I had to bum a Catholic priest in town for bus fare back to Chicago.

Conclusion

Even a man who works on Skid Row is condemned to poverty. In this industrial society where occupational status and wealth mainly determine a man's respect, Skid Row men not only have the worst jobs and the lowest pay, but they are also considered less than human.

Notes

[1]By August of 1973 only eleven temporary agencies were in business in the Madison area.

[2]For most agencies, about half of all employees for a day.

[3]Sometimes a man will take an advance with no intention of working in order to get a couple dollars.

[4]Wages paid a man are to the nearest quarter hour.

[5]There are some day labor jobs which pay $1.80 to $2.25 per hour. Companies pay $2.75 to $3.75 per hour for the same jobs, the labor office taking a commission.

Chapter V

The Derelicts of Justice

In this chapter, four major points are examined: 1) arrest, jail, and court for those in Skid Row; 2) duties and services of the Skid Row police; 3) how police view Skid Row; and 4) how Skid Row men view police, jail and court.

Arrest, Jail, and Court

When a policeman believes a Skid Row man to be inebriated, the man is searched. If the man has a wallet, his identification is recorded and the wallet is returned to him. The "convicted" person is then escorted to the rear of the patrol wagon. A man may be crowded inside with sometimes as many as fourteen other men (normal occupancy is six, no more than eight). Not seldom, police driving "bum wagons" wait until they have a full load (which could take up to an hour) before proceeding to the station. This undoubtedly invites a problem for the bladders of those individuals who have imbibed heavily. If a man is arrested east of Halsted Street, he is brought to the 1st District Police Headquarters at 11th and State. If he is west of Halsted, he is taken to the 12th District Police Station on Monroe and Racine.

Following arrival at the 1st District, the arrested climb out of the wagon and are marched in procession to the elevator which transfers them to the 11th floor lock-up. The 12th District lock-up is on ground level. A door (fashioned of bars) is unlocked to admit prisoners who must stand while each man is called forward to be interrogated by a policeman behind a counter. "What is your name, age, height, eye color, hair color, weight? In what state were you born? Where are you now living? Have you been drinking?" For a "bum" this last question is a mere formality before jail. The information taken, a prisoner turns over money and/or other valuables for police supervision and is given a receipt designating such property, the date, the arresting officer, and found charge. Prisoners arrested for "Drunk and Disorderly" retain their wallets, tobacco and other belongings. This entire booking procedure lasts ten to fifteen minutes for six to fifteen Skid Row "winos."

Cells are the next destination for the prisoners. The turnkey generally separates blacks from whites by placing them in different cells. Each cell has two wooden or steel planks (2 ft. X 7 ft., 2 1/2 ft. off floor) on opposite walls. A toilet (affluent niceties of seat and paper are absent), and sink (cold water only) are centered against the wall facing the heavy sliding iron-bar door. The guards place three to six men in each cell measuring 7 ft. X 15 ft. Only two men are able to sleep on the bare wooden or steel slats. The other men must retire on the cold cement floor. Fluorescent lights in the corridor glare continuously. Insects (remarkably adapted to the often filthy jail conditions) along with cigarettes and interaction with other cellmates afford the only outlets from boredom.

At 4:55 A.M. each prisoner, through the bars of his cell, is handed a piece of baloney between two slices of tasteless white bread and two ounces of coffee in a paper container. At 5:15 A.M. the prisoners arrested for public intoxication are taken from their cells to the desk inside the lock-up where, upon presentation of their endorsed receipt, money and valuables are returned. Then every prisoner is handcuffed to another inmate. After this, all are led to the elevators which place them on the first floor near the south end of the building. From here they are herded into large police transportation vehicles (designed to hold twenty-eight men not too uncomfortably). These take the Skid Row men to the 12th District Police Station on Monroe and Racine. Upon arrival (6:00 A.M.) the police direct the prisoners upstairs to the court where handcuffs are removed. The arrested are then shoved into a room (known to most Skid Rowers as the bullpen) adjacent to the courtroom. The bullpen

58

is 30 ft. X 12 ft. into which all fifty to seventy-five men from the 1st District are placed. There are no chairs in this room—just floor. In one corner there is a toilet (again without the customary seat and paper). Also, in an entrance area set off by bars between the court and bullpen, there is a sink, but prisoners are denied access to it. A trustee or two is allowed to give water to any man who asks for a drink. Inside the bullpen the majority of the men are quite friendly with one another sharing conversation and cigarettes. Space is so limited that only one half to four fifths are able to sit down. The rest stand. The prisoners are kept here for one and a half hours to one hour and forty-five minutes, when at 7:30 A.M. to 7:45 A.M. the men are ushered into the south area of the courtroom. After their names are called, they are placed in the north section of seats in the order in which they are to appear before the judge. When the arrested of the 1st District are suitably arranged, 12th District prisoners are brought upstairs from a bullpen on the first floor (in which they were placed at 5:00 A.M.) into the bullpen on the second floor previously occupied by the 1st District group. From here they are called out individually and seated in the south seating area in the same way as the 1st District prisoners. In general, the combined time for both moves is fifteen to twenty-five minutes, and is usually completed by 8:00 A.M. The next forty-five to sixty minutes are spent waiting for the judge to make his appearance. The one hundred to one hundred and thirty prisoners may converse, smoke or even leave their seats for short intervals, but must stay within the courtroom. At about 9:00 A.M., before the judge enters, a bailiff shouts, "Hear ye, hear ye. This court is now in session. Remove your hats and put out your cigarettes." A sign in the judge's quarters admonishes against "vulgar language." After taking his chair, the judge tries those arraigned by the 12th District first, and then proceeds to those from the 1st District. Seven names are called by an officer. The seven men called must acknowledge their presence by replying "here" and then line up in front of the judge (three or four in the front, the others behind them).

The judge looks over the faces of the accused and asks, "Do any of you need help?" Sometimes he will notice a man who has appeared too religiously at court. His honor gives him a twenty-one day vacation at government expense in the hoosegow. If a man appears physically ill from alcohol, he will normally be sent to Bridewell (a penal institution where he may receive medical care). In a few cases when a man is seriously ill, he will be sent to Cook County Hospital or Veteran's Hospital. Men with "emotional problems" are sent to Illinois State Hospital. Only between four and ten men are detained on any given day. So normally a man appears before the judge and receives his freedom in a matter of seconds. The entire Call Court takes no more than twenty to thirty minutes. Most Skid Row men prefer this form of abbreviated justice, because with little sleep, and anxious from boredom, they believe the faster they get out the better. Many Skid Rowers feel the presiding judge has some good qualities, e.g., he gives a warning before he sentences a "tramp." He scolds, "If I see you here next week, you'd better bring your toothbrush."

Duties and Services of the Police

Justice for Skid Row men is a subterfuge to punish said "deviants" for their desecration of the dominant moral order of which the foremost components are work, the nuclear family, and success. The custom of police jailing Skid Rowers is effected under the laws on drunk and disorderly conduct or, less often, vagrancy. These altars of justice are set forth in the Municipal Codes of Chicago.

193-1 A person commits disorderly conduct when he knowingly . . .
(g) Appears in any public place manifestly under the influence of alcohol, narcotics or other drugs, not therapeutically administered, to the degree that he may endanger himself or other persons or property, or annoy persons in his vicinity.

193-1.2 (a) It shall be unlawful for any person to drink any alcoholic liquor as defined by law on any public way or in or about any motor vehicle upon a public way in the city.

193-3 All persons who are idle and dissolute, or who go about begging; all persons who use any shell game, sleight-of-hand or juggling trick, or other unlawful game to cheat, defraud, or unlawfully obtain money or other valuable things; pilferers; confidence men; common drunkards; common night walkers; persons lewd, wanton, or lascivious in speech or behavior; common brawlers; persons who are habitually neglectful of their employment or their calling, and do not lawfully provide for themselves or for the support of their families; and all persons who are idle or dissolute and who neglect all lawful business, and who habitually misspend their time by frequenting houses of ill-fame or gambling houses; all persons lodging in or found in the night time in sheds, barns, or unoccupied buildings or lodging in the open air, and not giving a good account of themselves; and all persons who are known to be thieves, burglars, or pickpockets, either by their own confession or otherwise, or by having been convicted of larceny, burglary, or other crimes against the laws of the state punishable by imprisonment in the state prison or in a house of correction of any city, and having no lawful means of support, are habitually found prowling around any steamboat landing, railroad depot, banking institution, broker's office, place of public amusement, auction room, store, shop, or crowded public way, public conveyance, or at any public gathering or assembly, or lounging about any court room, private dwelling houses, or are found in any house of ill-fame or gambling house, are hereby declared to be vagabonds, and shall be fined not to exceed one hundred dollars for each offense. (amend. Coun. J. 12-21-39. p. 1396.)

It does not tax the imagination to understand the consequences of these vague laws for men on Skid Row. Albeit, these prefigure police responses toward the men. Interviews with twenty-six policemen assigned to the Skid Row detail yield the following data. Outside of their professional opinion, Skid Row policemen lack sensitivity for and knowledge of this social area. Of those surveyed, none has ever related, or made attempt to convey, an impression that he would seriously give second thought to associating in an unofficial capacity with "derelicts." Police relate to the "Skid Row deviants" only as a requisite to their work. The duties of the police department on Skid Row center around arrest and detention (this excludes businesses). Most policemen view their mechanical involvement with Skid Row as not befitting their proper role as policemen. For them, Skid Row must be policed because of its location in their district. Yet police, who by fate of job display their talents on Skid Row, often mouth humane rationales for this work, e.g.:

When they can't help themselves, we help them.

We protect them by trying to keep them out of trouble.

We give them a place to sleep at night. We save lives in the cold weather.

They're better off here.

We get 'em off the street and give 'em shelter and something to eat.

We help the bums by putting them in jail for a night.

We protect them against themselves.

We arrest them for their own well being.

We take 'em to the hospital if they're sick.

No doubt these statements have some foundation in fact, but further analysis of police-Skid Row relations offers broader interpretation. Actually, police overstate their usefulness to Skid Row and delude themselves that their tactics of inflicting hardships are noble humanitarian gestures on the men's behalf.

Police services on Skid Row consist of transferring the sick or dead and locking up "drunks" for safe keeping, to protect them from bad weather and/or themselves. Police are relegated the onerous chore of removing the sick or dead in the "meat wagon" (paddy wagon) to a hospital and/or the morgue. Most such referrals occur through the hotels or courts. Under circumstances in which a guest

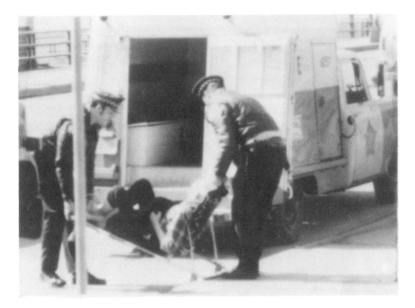

Police transport a sick man from his hotel to a hospital.

in a Skid Row hotel is in need of medical attention or has died, a hotel manager usually contributes a few dollars to each officer for his help in order to insure future cooperation. Police must also chauffeur those individuals whom the court recognizes as in dire need of hospital care.

In the middle of winter, men drunk and unable to walk are put in jail. Understandably, some men are rescued who would otherwise die in the cold. Men in a drunken stupor are taken to the police station to protect them from getting jackrolled and/or becoming the object of someone's aggressive frustrations.

Daily, between one hundred and one hundred and thirty men are ceremoniously imprisoned in a lawful observance which assigns various punitive measures and denies constitutional rights (trial, lawyer). The height of absurdity is the opinion of many Skid Row policemen that, "Jail doesn't bother these guys; they don't care." Contrary to this police convention, jail is painfully boring—an anathema to Skid Rowers. Other than apathy, what recourse have

63

they? Furthermore, usually only a small percentage (one to four) of those (one hundred to one hundred and thirty) Skid Row men arrested for being drunk require medical treatment. All men apprehended for this "offense" walk unassisted into the lock-up[1] where they, under police questioning, give coherent replies. What is more preposterous than the belief of policemen which upholds throwing "bums" in jail is granting them an invaluable act of charity, is that often a few in urgent need of a doctor must survive jail until the morning Call Court.[2]

Police View of Skid Row

Police-bum social interaction consists of these forms of behavior. Police are paternalistic, regarding men on Skid Row as harmless derelicts who cannot take care of themselves, children who need their protection. The Skid Row man becomes a subordinate, whose principal activity is venerating policemen.

A trustee at the 12th District Police Station

An arrangement between police and trustees is a microcosm of this relationship. Each morning before the Skid Row men are placed in the bullpen, the jailkeeper asks two to six regulars at the police station if they want to work. As an incentive, trustees are exempt from appearing in court. Such work includes giving coffee to prisoners, and janitorial tasks (scrubbing floors, emptying waste paper baskets, hosing down cells). Also on the work list is shining shoes, running errands, and washing the private cars of policemen. These "derelicts" must bend and scrape to police demands.

After four hours of work, the trustees are released at approximately the same time as the prisoners from the Call Court. Another example is recounted by a patrolman:

> Went in the McCoy Hotel to get a man who was dead for about two weeks. It had maggots and worms and smelled so damn bad I deputized three onlookers in the hotel. The rooms are so small that two of those guys couldn't get in the cubicle to carry the body out, so this one big fellow went in and picked up the corpse, folded it up and got outside the room with it and put it on the stretcher. When the smell hit him he started throwing up all over! The other two helpers carried it down and put it in our paddy wagon. Believe me, it was so bad we gave each of the men thirty-five cents!

Asked if anything could (or should) be done to improve the conditions of Skid Row, many police concluded that nothing could help it.

> It's up to the individual to better himself.
>
> I don't know. If we get rid of it, it would have to go somewhere else.
>
> It's not a police problem.
>
> Nothing can be done.
>
> It's up to the men themselves if they want to straighten themselves out.

65

Fix the flophouses.

It's hard to say if anyone can improve the conditions.

No, they don't want anything done.

No, if ya knock it down they just move someplace else.

Nothing; they're hopeless.

Tear it down.

No, it's a tourist attraction.

Correct psychiatric problems.

Can't do anything for them; they're through and will never be anything.

Shouldn't let them lay all over.

A specific law for jackrollers. Can't put men up for fifteen years for stealin' 45¢. We need thirty to sixty day sentences.

Increase our patrols.

No, definitely.

An honest answer is no.

Everything that could be done is being done.

They have to do it themselves and get off the street and get a job.

Nothing can be done except to arrest them. It's like taking care of little children. They're like little kids.

They could try to do somethin', but these guys don't want anything. They're like kids; ya have ta take care of them. They don't want to work. They get assistance checks and hit the first tavern and blow it all in one night. Social agencies have been trying for years. Nothing can be done unless they do it them-selves. They don't even have control over their own bowel movements.

To these policemen, Skid Row is an incorrectable pathology— the result of individual failure to accept responsibility in our society.

The following are the reasons the policemen give as to why they think men are on Skid Row.

Family problems.

They can't put up with the outside world; they don't want to get off Skid Row, and wine.

Most of them are from broken families.

Problems; they have all types. They left home. Couldn't take it.

Personal problems.

I'd say the big reason is alcoholism. Then they have no home—there are some rich men on Skid Row saving their money.

They couldn't adjust to their own problems.

Something happened and they started drinking. They tend to go to their own kind.

Problems too difficult to face.

They got problems they can't handle so they drink.

They're trying to get away from something—like marriage problems.

Alcoholism.

Their own fault.

Failure.

Skid Row is survival of the fittest. It's an easy way of life. They live off people by stealing.

They got psychological problems.

It's women. Ninety percent of 'em got screwed by broads. Or marital problems—women are always somehow connected.

They want to get away. Family doesn't care anymore.

They were born bums.

Emotional problems.

Personal problems, like their wife died. I met a guy the other day who came to Skid Row twenty years ago after his wife died.

Most are alcoholics.

They live like animals; no control over themselves. They don't care about anything but wine. They've got no worries down here.

Family trouble.

Down and out of a job, the vast majority gave up the rat race of life. This is the only place where they can get food and shelter.

They're weak individuals who resorted to alcohol to solve their problems.

Skid Row View of Police, Jail, and Court

In comparison, Skid Row men do not perceive the police and judge as their protectors and benefactors. Ninety informants from Skid Row were asked to comment on their experiences with police, jail and the court system. Twenty-six percent expressed overall approval, or acceptance, of this machinery of justice. The others criticized police brutality and corruption, jail conditions, and/or restraints on their legal rights. The following statements are not intended to prove or refute such practices by the police and/or the judge. Additions, deletions, exaggerations and modifications of common spoken experiences accrue as a type of oral tradition on Skid Row. The preponderance of answers from Skid Row men not only fall within the above-mentioned categories (brutality, etc.), but are also very uniform in content. Thus, if statements of any men are fabrications, they are at least an indication of cultural attitudes. Some of the men's comments are as follows:

They're the biggest jackrollers in the city of Chicago.

68

They'll go through your pockets; if you have ten dollars, kiss it goodbye.

Greedy as anyone could be. They don't always wait till you're drunk. They'll go in your pockets and if there's any money, they'll just keep it.

Dirty thieving bastards—rob people. In July 1969 they robbed me of $180.

If you act right you won't get the shit kicked out of you.

Some are good, some are brutal. They'll hit anyone.

They hit me in the arm with a club. It did something to my nerve. I could hardly move it for a month.

If you get nasty, police get nasty.

The author observed many sadistic acts by Skid Row police. Many of these policemen tend to shun bodily contact with "those dirty bums who never change their clothes or take a bath." In making an arrest, policemen use different means to prod a drunk (who has passed out on the street) into the paddy wagon. Occasionally, a man will undergo the brunt of a policeman's misanthropic aggressions. For example, many the fibula of an unconscious bum has yielded to a policeman's riot club. Hair when pulled by an officer also effectively aborts a state of drunkenness. The following is another example observed by the author.

One balmy summer night at 1:00 A.M., a man about forty-five years of age was staggering out of a bar (Jack Pot Inn) with an obese lady. When they reached the corner, the man made unmistakable sexual overtures toward the woman. Upon the sidewalk, they embraced with much intent. Not long after, two policemen in a squad car pulled up and interrupted their amorous activity by placing them under arrest. Another squad car stopped. After they put the prisoners in the car, the police went over to joke about the incident with the late arriving officers. With some temerity the man got out of the patrol car and began to walk away, giving the policemen an obscene gesture. One of the policemen shouted, "You goddamn fucker, where do you think you're going?!" He charged after the man, grabbed him and pushed him into a parked car. He then pulled out his club and used it to slam the man's head five times into the hood of the car. For almost three more minutes he roughed up the man, until finally he kneed him and literally shoved him back in the car.

Jail is a monument to police inability to understand the precarious lives of Skid Row men. When speaking on the subject of jail, most men from Skid Row will mention its ungenial conditions.

Ya get no blankets, just steel bunks. Even then, alot of times its so crowded ya have ta sleep on the cement floor.

Jail is dirty and it's got bugs all over.

They herd you into a bullpen at five in the morning when you're sick. There's hardly room to sit down and you're there to nine o'clock.

Just the other day, a man in jail moaned all night; the next morning when they came to get him out, he was dead.

A Skid Row man is not innocent until proven guilty; he is guilty by arrest. His only defense against a policeman is obedience, politeness, and subservience.

They'll pick you up even when you aint been drinking! I got off day labor, cashed my check in a bar. As I walked out I got arrested.

A couple days ago, I was walking down the street. These cops were arresting some drunks. They saw me and said, "Get in." I wasn't even drunk. I was so damn mad and raised so much disturbance they threw me in a cell with the coloreds.

When ya get arrested, ya can't say nothing. The next morning in court, ya don't get a lawyer even if they put ya in Bridewell for a month.

Many Skid Row men detest the police and jail, yet they passively condone proceedings of the Skid Row court. Subjugated by the formidable structures of law enforcement, the short duration of the Call Court is to them the best of available alternatives.

Police records indicate that men from Skid Row are rarely arrested for anything other than drunk and disorderly conduct. Nevertheless, jackrolling and fighting, along with numerous other unlawful undertakings, are common on Skid Row. There are several reasons for this discrepancy. Although not appreciated, jackrolling and fighting are almost natural (daily) occurrences to most Skid Rowers, and are not usually police matters. Feelings of passivity (not wanting to get involved), fear (because of previous arrests), or animosity toward police tend to discourage many Skid Row men from approaching them for assistance. Finally, police indifference to "derelicts" is another influencing factor. For example, one evening a thin man in his middle forties limped in the door and up the stairs to the front desk at the 12th District Police Station. He was dressed only in tattered pants and worn shoes. He was out of breath and sweating profusely. The man's right cheek and back had lacerations and abrasions. He told the sergeant behind the desk that he had just been jackrolled in an alley about a block away. He spoke with desperation, "Them niggers took everything I got—my money, my veteran's card, and beat me up. And they're still in that alley—I'll show you where!" The officer interrupted him, "I don't know of a policeman in the city who would leave his desk to chase after jackrollers. You need a patrol car and we don't have one here." When the man persisted, the policeman with sarcasm in his voice said, "Will you shut up, stupid." The man remarked, "If I were stupid, sir, I wouldn't be here reporting this. You're the police; you've got to help me!" Finally the desk sergeant yelled, "Aw go on. Get out of here!" Angry, frustrated, weeping, the Skid Row man left.

Summary

Policemen view arresting Skid Row men as a humanitarian duty: "locking the men up for safe keeping." Policemen are paternalistic.

They treat men on Skid Row like children in need of their help. Every day over one hundred men are arrested for drunk and disorderly and locked in jail. The only help they receive is a cold cement floor, bars, and long hours of waiting until they are released the next morning in Call Court.

Even though police perform a number of services which are helpful to some men on Skid Row, for the most part the police work becomes a ritual which serves dominant societal ethics by subtly rendering hardships on Skid Row "deviants".

Notes

[1]A jailkeeper cannot accept anyone who is unconscious.

[2]Although the police department stipulates that men with serious injuries or whose health has appreciably deteriorated are to be taken to Cook County Hospital after arrest, Skid Row police officers are not always successful in diagnosing the medical problems of the prisoners.

Chapter VI

Other Related Institutions

Bars

To mission directors a man on Skid Row is a sinner. To police he is lazy. Psychiatrists and counselors reduce him to a few personality disorders. Employment offices and second-hand stores gain from his poverty. Only in the bars on Skid Row does a tramp or bum have a sense of worth. A man with money can enjoy himself in these bars. Here he can pass the time drinking, talking, or sitting quietly without fear of getting jackrolled.

Skid Row bars have many attractions such as color televisions, jukeboxes (playing mostly country-western music), pool tables (a quarter a game), cuspidors, and, in some bars, women.

About ten of the forty-one bars in the Madison Skid Row area have a regular female clientele.[1] On crowded weekend nights only a couple of these bars have more than fifteen or twenty women. Most of them usually have no more than two or three women at any time. The women do not work for bars as prostitutes, although they will at times cater to a man's prurient wants for about ten dollars. The creative abilities of some of these women are legendary with men on Skid Row. A man spoke of one such experience. While drinking in a bar he propositioned a woman to go to his room with him. As they left he bought a bottle. They drank in his room until the man passed out. When he awoke the lady was gone and the money in his wallet was missing.

Women who frequent Skid Row bars are largely American In-

73

Legion Tavern

dians and southern whites. Either they live on Skid Row in one of the hotels which accomodate women, or in apartments throughout the city, usually not farther than five miles from West Madison Street.

All Skid Row bars sell a wide variety of liquors: beer, gin, vodka, wine, whiskey, etc. For most customers drinking at the bar, beer is consumed most frequently, sometimes with a shot. In the last three years liquor prices have risen markedly: 15¢ to 20¢ for a small glass of draught beer, 25¢ to 35¢ for a large glass of beer, 40¢ to 50¢ for a 12 ounce bottle of beer, and 55¢ to 70¢ for a pint of wine. White or dark port wine is the largest selling carry-out. For an extra nickel some bars give two cigarettes with a pint of wine. Smoking tobaccos, candy bars, Tums, aspirins, Bromo-Selzer, 10¢ packages of potato chips, pretzels, popcorn, and nuts, are available for purchase at any bar on Skid Row.

The major function of Skid Row bars is to fulfill the social needs of the men. Bartenders usually talk with the steady customers, knowing many of them by name. Some men have their checks mailed to

74

Skid Row bars often advertise their liquor prices.

a bar so they can get cash or drinks whenever they want. Many of the bars keep ledgers and charge a few dollars for the service. Loud, friendly, ribald joking is almost always evident among patrons in the bars. For instance, one afternoon in the Jack Pot Inn, a sixty year old woman was on her way to use the toilet when someone called, "Hey Patti! Do you wear a girdle?" She proudly lifted her dress to her shoulders to show a lack of undergarments. Everyone laughed.

If alcohol were a man's only concern, he could purchase a bottle and drink it on the street or in his hotel room for half the price of drinking in a bar. Individuals inside bars tend to drink slowly, taking thirty to forty-five minutes for a glass of beer. On the street it is not uncommon for an individual or a group to empty a pint of wine within a few minutes.

75

"Big" Rothchild's Bar

Lindy Grill

Short-Order Restaurants

In 1922 a ten cent meal could be obtained in many of the cheap restaurants along the main stem of Skid Row (Anderson, 1923). Today Skid Row restaurants are comparable to inexpensive restaurants or grills anywhere in the city. Prices are moderate, and the selection is not bad. Food and prices are posted on signs in all the restaurants on Skid Row—no menus. To insure, in part, faithful patrons, some restaurants accept welfare disbursing orders and sell "commutation tickets" for five dollars which entitle a bearer to $5.50 in food.

On Skid Row men don't give tips; it's unheard of. Although most Skid Row restaurants are dingy, the food is neither putrid nor deletrious to health.

Second-Hand Stores

Many men on Skid Row have defeating existences. They work daily pay or odd jobs for a while and slowly accumulate material possessions—shoes, clothing, radios. Eventually they take to drinking heavily, discontinue working, and must sell anything and everything they own to get money for a drink.

As of 1972, eleven second-hand stores (two of these are more accurately classified as junk shops) operated in the Madison Skid Row area. In late 1973, six second-hand stores were left. No pawnshops are located on West Madison Street.

Laws and Their Effects

City laws seem to deter pawnshops from operating in the Madison Street Skid Row area. The annual fee for a pawnshop license is twelve hundred dollars, for a second-hand store the fee is thirty-five dollars. A pawnbroker cannot charge more than three percent per month for money advanced on personal property, and if the pawner defaults in the payment of interest on the money, normally the property pawned cannot be sold for one year.

The individual pawning an article must be given a "memorandum or note" indicating the article pawned, money loaned, rate of interest, the date, and his name. In addition to maintaining a book including the above information, the pawnshop is also required to make out a report each day of all property received on that day and forward it to the police. A second-hand dealer only has to keep a book designating information concerning purchases.

Inasmuch as most Skid Row men have property of no significant monetary value, and will sell anything for money to buy a jug when desperate for a drink, it is impractical for a shop owner to give a loan on an article of limited value when he can buy it for almost nothing. What is more, after a man has sold an article to a second-hand dealer, in order to redeem it he must pay three to five times as much as he got for it.

The Clientele

Men on Skid Row not only stock the second-hand stores with merchandise, but are also their principal customers. One informant explains, "We're the losers all around no matter how you look at it." This impression is evident in the comments of many Skid Row men.

A man down and out will sell his shoes, shirt, any fuckin' thing to get a drink.

Ya sell your jacket for a dollar for a pint of wine. Ya go back, if it aint been sold ya'll have to pay like eight bucks for it.

I went in Sam's with Detroit Johnny. We had this shopping bag with all kinds of stuff. I mean shirts, underwear, socks, pants or so. All we got was a dollar. Everything was laundered; it hadn't been worn, and just stuffed in the bag.

I sold a suitcase plus a suit. I got one dollar out of it. The suit alone was worth forty-five dollars. What are ya going to do? They have ya over a barrel.

A drinking man'll sell anything he's got for almost nothing. I had a forty dollar camera, a suitcase and all my clothes. I was offered two dollars an' fifty cents. I needed the money so I let them go.

Any of these places will only give ya a quarter for a pair of glasses. It'll cost ya a dollar to a dollar fifty to get 'em again.

Second-hand dealers have refined finagling for the merchandise they buy from needy men. Most Skid Row men who have sold property at second-hand stores have had experiences much like the following.

I was broke and had to get a drink somehow. I had these brand new twenty-two dollar black leather boots, so I go into Uncle Ed's, shaking an' nervous an' needing a drink. He saw me an' says, 'What do ya want?!' I pulled off one of my boots an' showed him it. He took one look at me, shaking hands, trembling nerves, looked at my boot an' said, 'Eh, how much ya want for 'em?' I told him four bucks. 'Nope. Can't use 'em. Got too many already. 'Sides, they aint worth four bucks.' I put my boot back on an' started to leave. As I opened the door, he said, 'I'll let ya have 75¢ for 'em.' I told him he was outa his cotton-pickin' mind. Then he told me to go an' find another place that'll give four dollars, let alone two dollars. As I opened the door his voice became more gentle an' he said, 'I'll give ya a dollar for 'em.' I turned an' said, 'Two dollars an' ya got yourself a pair of boots.' He said, 'Get yourself a pair of relievers.'[2] I got two dollars an' a pair of cob-web relievers. I went across the street an' got a bottle before I fell over.

Feeling exploited, Skid Row men usually speak with bitterness and resentment about the owners of second-hand stores.

They got money signs in both eyeballs. What the hell, they make a living off of poor tramps.

Just like body lice, they're parasites on the bum.

Why Men Use Second-Hand Stores

A variety of goods are sold at the second-hand stores on West Madison, such as alarm clocks, glasses, paperback books, pants, shirts, shoes, coats, socks, nail clippers, ties, hats, lunch pails, tools, walking canes, radios, watches, rings, old cameras, pots and pans, suitcases, and padlocks. Clothes are among the fastest selling items. Prices are cheaper by far then most stores in other parts of the city.

Socks	$ .15 —	$ .25
Work pants	1.00 —	1.50
Dress pants	2.00 —	4.00
Shirts	.50 —	2.50
Shoes	3.00 —	10.00
Underwear	.25 —	.50
Coats	5.00 —	15.00

Not only are prices low, but there are other reasons for Skid Row men to use the second-hand stores. On Skid Row it costs as much to have clothes laundered as to buy used clothes at a second-hand store and throw away the soiled wear. A man can get a shirt, pants, socks, and underwear for under two dollars at the second-hand stores. Rates for the same items at the only laundry on Madison (about 80% of whose customers are from areas other than Skid Row) are: pants $1.00, shirts 50¢, socks 25¢, underwear 25¢. For a man to wash and dry his own clothes he must walk to a laundromat on the 1100 block of Madison, pay 55¢ for machines, buy soap, and wait about one and a half hours.[3] For many Skid Row men, owning few clothes, this is too much trouble.

Skid Row missions give clothes, shoes, jackets, etc. to the men. Undoubtedly this damages the business of second-hand stores. Yet the practice of some missions which requires the men to attend services, and others which distribute a limited selection of clothing at appointed hours only, must influence a man's decision to buy his clothes at a second-hand store.

Recipients of public aid are mailed checks for clothing—disability $6.88 each month, general assistance $27.00 every six months. If a recipient mismanages this money, thereafter he is given a disbursing order, which is made out to a clothing store. The vender must send the order to the Department of Public Aid in Springfield which issues a check for the clothes.

In conclusion, the second-hand stores of West Madison Street

A Secondhand Store

perform important social functions, because they enable men who are broke and in immediate need of a drink to sell their belongings and get money for a bottle. At the same time these second-hand stores offer the men on Skid Row merchandise like clothing at somewhat inexpensive prices.

Waller Public Bath

At 19 South Peoria, a half block south of Madison Street, is the last of the public bathhouses operated by the Chicago Park District; others in Chicago have closed over the years due to shortages in attendance. Before a man is allowed to shower here, he must pick up a ticket, free of charge, at the Municipal Reading Room. Towels are not supplied. An average of fifty Skid Row men use this facility each day in the summer. When the weather gets cold the attendance drops to about ten men per day.

The Waller Public Bath

82

Municipal Reading Room

Funded by the city's Department of Human Resources, the Reading Room at 925 West Madison is managed by George Cooper, a minister of the Episcopal Church, and his staff of two or three men. Cooper runs the reading room under what he calls the "open door policy." Any man on the street may use the building as a shelter while it is open eight hours a day five days a week, and on Saturday from eight-thirty to noon. The Reading Room's motto echoes this policy: "Do something for your fellow man, even if it is only leaving him alone."

The Municipal Reading Room has two floors: one with a television for "senior citizens only," and the other with various reading materials (newspapers and used books donated by the Chicago Public Library), and a washroom where men may shave. Up to four hundred men a day use the Reading Room. Theft of razors is a minor source of irritation to Cooper, but twenty-three years of

The Municipal Reading Room

experience have taught him this: "If a man comes in for a shave, I let him have a razor, but he leaves his shirt with me."

The Reading Room has only a few rules: "No drunks and no bottles allowed inside." Sleeping, spitting, and smoking are also not allowed. Any man who disobeys the rules is asked to leave. In September, 1973, the Municipal Reading Room was moved to 12 South Peoria. Reverend Cooper died in 1977 and, sadly, the Reading Room was closed shortly thereafter.

Starr and Garter Theatre

This old theatre once saw the glamorous days of burlesque and vaudeville. By 1971, the Starr and Garter featured only three or four rather dull movies on any given day. Shows started at eight o'clock A.M. and continued to ten o'clock P.M. Price of admission was a dollar. Skid Row men used the Starr Theatre to pass the time watching movies, quietly drinking a bottle, sleeping, and as a shelter in bad weather. Also the men's washroom had, for those so inclined, its own sources of amusement. In 1971 the Starr and Garter was torn down and a parking lot built in its place.

Pool Hall

The Monterrey Pool Hall has six worn dusty tables. Most customers are only interested in buying candy, potato chips, and soft drinks anyway. Frank, the owner, is seventy years old and has been in business here since 1952. "I don't make much off of here," says Frank, "only ten to fifteen dollars a week. I get social security, too." Over the years Frank has built up a small but dependable number of friends who pay him a visit and enjoy a soda.

Barber College

Some men on Skid Row recall a time when Madison Street had as many as seven barber colleges. Only one has endured in this area. Owner Joe Palopoli talks of happier days:

"Years ago I had forty to sixty students. Now I'm lucky if I have two or three." Students pay a fee of $670. They receive instruction as they cut the hair of those men who value a $1.25 haircut more than their appearance. A haircut anywhere else in the city is three dollars or more.

Groceries and Delicatessens

Three small grocery stores and one delicatessen were in business in the Madison area during my study. Many men on Skid Row, without access to a stove and ice box, must buy goods which do not need to be cooked or refrigerated. This is reflected in the products sold in these stores. Items such as fruit, sandwiches, cookies, doughnuts, candy, milk, and orange juice, are, by sales, the most popular. These grocery stores also sell many canned foods. While there is less demand for this merchandise, it may be stored on a shelf for an indefinite amount of time without spoiling.

A small grocery store near Madison and Halsted

Currency Exchange
1000 West Madison

Eighteen percent of the clients are men from Madison Street Skid Row. The rest come from factories in the area surrounding Madison. The usual types of checks cashed at the currency exchange by Skid Row men are pension, annuity, welfare, veterans assistance, and social security.

Chicago Alcoholic Treatment Center
3026 South California Avenue

The Chicago Alcoholic Treatment Center is a seventy-two bed, in-patient facility for male "alcoholics." The center is supported by corporate funds of the city. Seven to eight thousand men have been treated at CATC since 1957. A psychologist at CATC states that about eight percent of its patients are from Skid Row. Men are allowed to go through the in-patient program only once. The program lasts an average of thirty-seven days. After a man has completed the program, he may return as an out-patient for limited group therapy, Alcoholics Anonymous meetings, etc.

Notes

[1]Skid Row bars may be further distinguished: The Mexican Village is a bar for Spanish-speaking persons from the Skid Row area, and more often, other neighborhoods, and two bars west of Racine Avenue have black patrons not from Madison Skid Row.
[2]Relievers is a Skid Row term for the dilapidated shoes given to a man as replacements for his shoes which he sells to the second-hand store.
[3]A few Skid Row hotels have washers and dryers for their guests.

Chapter VII

And The Rich Shall Inherit The Earth

When flies accumulate there's some kind of filth attracting them. So you get rid of the garbage and you get rid of the flies. Winos aren't going to come around culture and beauty and cleanliness.

> Park Livingston
> President, West Central Assoc.
> Mercantile Bank of Chicago

In life you can't have love without hate, joy without sorrow, or Kenilworth[1] without Skid Row. Urban Renewal should start with Kenilworth.

> S. Taylor
> Skid Row Bum

The West Central Association, organized in 1926 to represent the interests of the principal property owners of the Near West Side of Chicago, has been among the leading proponents of the elimination of Madison Street Skid Row. Its expressed concern is to "help rehabilitate and redevelop the West Central area."[2] The "slum neighborhood" of Skid Row will be removed from the Loop area and replaced by "an orderly and highly developed tax paying industrial district."[3] "Besides," says James Dow, executive director of the West Central Association, "why would anyone want to live there? We had a committee go into every hotel. I couldn't stand the odor."[4] In tearing down Skid Row, they seem to confuse their financial interests with a superficial intention to help the men who live there.

Many members of W.C.A. have vested interests in the Skid Row area. W.C.A. represents most of the businesses on the Near West Side, including twenty-one real estate companies and four banks. Among the members of the Board of Directors are representatives of the Holiday Inn-Chicago Downtown (a relatively new addition to Madison Street between Halsted Street and the Kennedy Express-way), the Madison-Canal Development Company (developers of the six block area of Skid Row between Clinton Street and the Kennedy Expressway), and the Mid City Bank of Chicago situated at the corner of Madison and Halsted.

To the West Central Association, Skid Row offers a "central location with immediate access to every type of business services and customers; the unique convergence of all forms of transportation . . .; . . . land for growth . . ."[5] W.C.A.'s main objective is to use Skid Row to extend the Loop area of Downtown, to make Skid Row a complement to the other side of the Eisenhower Expressway. "We aim to rebuild the city, get rid of the rubble and the blight," says Park Livingston. To the businessmen of the W.C.A., Skid Row is a means to an end, and the only thing standing between them and pay dirt is, as Livingston calls them, those "human derelicts who have lost their reason and their dignity."

Many West Central businessmen are capitalizing on the benefits of Urban Renewal projects on Skid Row. "The sound of bulldozers leveling a site. Hammers ringing against steel. Glass building grow-ing out of the compost of vacant lot and slum. New construction—new expansion—new pride."[6] Indeed, each of the four area banks has spent enormous sums to renovate its facilities and construct new buildings. The Mercantile National Bank's interior is especially attractive with its "butternut woodwork and ebony cages. Its stair-case, which is laid with ceramic tile purchased in Italy and installed piece by piece has won awards, as has its beautiful outdoor sign."[7] Edwin M. Bakwin, Chairman of the board of Mid City National Bank, boasts that "Skid Row is definitely finished. The people left the area because the things that made them stay are being erased. We have started to see the change, our bank deposits, for example, have increased twenty percent in just the last two years."[8]

The West Central Association's monthly luncheons at the Holiday Inn on Madison and Halsted best exemplify their conception of "rehabilitating" Skid Row. After drinking at an open bar, members view anything from a show of women modeling the latest styles in clothes to slides of plans for new buildings at demolished sites.

Urban Renewal

A locked door stops any man on the street from making an unwanted entrance into the building. In a back room of the Urban Renewal Madison-Canal office at 651 West Madison Street, there is a ping-pong table for employees. In addition to this pastime, the Urban Renewal office was established on Skid Row to promote community relations. For years, the Department of Urban Renewal has maintained an image of concern for the men. Under section 314 of the Housing Act of 1954, a Demonstration Grant was awarded the City of Chicago to study living conditions on Skid Row and to aid the Department of Urban Renewal in eliminating it and preventing its recurrence elsewhere. In its application for the grant, the D.U.R. stated,

> by mapping out a course of action that enlists the collective effort of health, welfare, philanthropic, police, judicial, and employment facilities, the urban renewal program offers an unparalleled opportunity to make positive progress toward the elimination of this worst section of our society . . . (Newman, 1961:1)

For the D.U.R. Skid Row is just another project, but one that differs from any of their others. A "normal" project tends to have a much larger staff which is divided into a rehabilitation staff, a relocation staff, and a demolition staff.

A normal rehabilitation staff searches for building violations with the aid of building and fire department inspectors and gives notice to the owners as to what improvements are to be made. Urban Renewal's standards are higher than those of the city's building department; failure to meet these standards could result in court intervention or loss of the building. Because a normal project is federally funded, loans of up to $14,500 with 3% interest rates are available to property owners to help them meet Urban Renewal's standards.

Twenty percent of the buildings in an area must be structurally deteriorated to justify Urban Renewal's activity there. The D.U.R. forms a Community Conservation Committee, members of which are recommended by the mayor. This committee and the local P.T.A., Chamber of Commerce, alderman, and other civic groups work with the D.U.R. in deciding the future of their neighborhood. The area coordinator (manager of the project for the D.U.R.) attends all community meetings and keeps the Urban Renewal office and the community informed of each other's activities. Invitations to attend D.U.R. meetings and hearings are mailed to "community members."

The Madison-Canal Urban Renewal office has no rehabilitation staff and no Community Conservation Committee because, as K. Marrin area coordinator says, "We are a total clearance project. None of these buildings can be saved. Besides, we do not receive federal funds so we don't have to meet federal requirements."

All Urban Renewal projects have relocation staffs which function in two capacities: they tend to the immediate social needs of the residents and assist in the relocation of residents and businesses. K. Marrin calls her office a "funneling counseling service." A counselor comes in periodically to talk to the men who may want to find their families, receive welfare, "dry out," etc. When men are evicted from a condemned hotel, the relocation staff finds them comparable hotels or other accomodations. For example, of the 430 men displaced from the two northeast blocks of the Madison-Canal area, only fifty to sixty of them, according to K. Marrin, were relocated into senior citizen homes off Skid Row. Some of the four hundred and thirty men went to the city's Alcoholic Treatment Center and mission programs, but most were moved to other flophouses in the area. In relocating businesses on Skid Row, the D.U.R. pays moving expenses and, if a business is unable to pay, also advances the first month's rent at the new location. Urban Renewal tries to move people to places they want to go, yet they try to "motivate people to live in a particular area," especially in other projects involving families. "We're familiar with all the ethnic communities in Chicago. We like to relocate the people into areas where it would be easiest for them to live."

All Urban Renewal projects, including Madison-Canal, have demolition staffs which supervise the acquisition of each building, the bidding for land, the signing of contracts, and the wrecking.

In September of 1966, the West Central Association presented the city and the D.U.R. with their plan to clear a 15.5 acre, six block area from Clinton Street to the Kennedy Expressway between Washington Boulevard and Monroe Street. Under the provisions of the Illinois Urban Renewal Consolidation Act of 1961, the D.U.R. designated the Madison-Canal area as a "Slum and Blighted Area," enabling them to use the city's powers of eminent domain to clear the land. Lewis W. Hill, Chicago's commissioner of Urban Renewal, said $18,497,200[10] would be required to buy and clear the eighty-nine existing buildings from the land. The plan was to sell the vacant land to developers for at least this amount, therefore making federal or city financial aid unnecessary.

Mayor Richard J. Daley set two requirements for the program: 1) that the rebuilding of the area must be planned as a whole, and 2) that "decent new homes" be found for the residents of Skid Row.[11] Ed Lally, assistant commissioner of the D.U.R., became project coordinator and attempted over a three year period to obtain federal aid for a half-way house. A study conducted by D.U.R. consultant Ronald C. Vanderkooi had proposed a half-way community which would house up to 2,000 men. When no funds were received, the project was reduced to a five story, forty unit efficiency pilot apartment building which was to receive funds under F.H.A. Program 236, a family housing program. A court injunction prevented construction of this building. Lally has since retired, and the plans have been forgotten.

Having the right to decide the type of structures to be built at a site, the D.U.R. specified that the six block complex, Place Du Sable, was to be an array of apartment buildings, offices, and restaurants. On December 5, 1968, D.U.R. commissioner Lewis W. Hill announced the developers chosen for the Place Du Sable

Project. This development firm, formed on October 17, 1968, was composed of Charles Swibel, a local real estate magnate; Wallace E. Johnson and Kemmons Wilson of Holiday Inns; Lloyd E. Clarke, President and Chief Executive Officer of Alodex Corporation; and M. L. Bartling Jr., Director of the U.S. Gypsum Urban Development Company.

Since 1968, the news media have repeatedly accused the Madison-Canal project of corruption. Swibel, for example, has been accused of conflict of interest because, while manipulating city sponsored real estate transactions, he serves as Chairman of the Chicago Housing Authority. Also, the partnership agreement between the four developers of the Place Du Sable held that "Swible was to be paid one million dollars only if the Madison-Canal Company bid was accepted. Swibel received this payment without making any investment of capital in the partnership or incurring any liability."[12]

All work on the Place Du Sable was halted when the General Services Administration, under the Federal Government, filed an order taking the north block of Madison Street between Jefferson and DesPlaines for a ten story social security building. Urban Renewal couldn't deliver the entire six blocks designated in the contract with the Madison-Canal Corporation. As a result the Madison-Canal Corporation rejected the contract, although they did retain one block between Madison and Clinton which they had already purchased. A glut of office space near the Loop appears to have made the original Place Du Sable project unattractive to the Madison-Canal Corporation. No plans for the development of the remaining four blocks have been accepted, although the City Council has given the D.U.R. the right to negotiate any new contracts. In any event, Urban Renewal expects to have the Skid Row area east of the Kennedy Expressway cleared by 1979.

In 1976 the D.U.R. initiated a plan to redevelop a 177.36 acre site west of the Kennedy Expressway to Ogden Avenue, and south of Lake Street to Madison and Monroe Streets. This project is already underway, and will eventually tear down all the Skid Row buildings west of the Kennedy Expressway. Also, the commercial businesses of the Fulton Market area will be forced to relocate.

Notes

[1]Kenilworth is a wealthy suburb of Chicago.

[2]*Growth and Improvement Through Bold Dynamic Moves*, a pamphlet of the West Central Association, 1964, p. 1.

[3]Pamphlet sent to businessmen who are prospective members of the West Central Association.

[4]Unless footnoted, all direct quotes in this chapter were taken from personal interviews by the author.

[5]Directory of the West Central Assoc., 1973-74, p. 4.

[6]Advertisement for the Mid City National Bank in the 1973-74 directory of the W.C.A., p. 1.

[7]*Growth and Improvement Through Bold Dynamic Moves*, p. 5.

[8]William Schaub, "Skid Row Fading From City Scene," *Chicago American*, Oct. 11, 1964, p. 31.

[10]*Growth and Improvement Through Bold Dynamic Moves*, p. 22.

[11]*Ibid.*

[12]Glendi Sampson and Dick Cheverton, *Chicago Today*, Jan. 16, 1970, p. 17.

Chapter VIII

Argot

Word of mouth is the primary mode of communication on Skid Row. This takes on further importance because socialization into Skid Row culture proceeds through accumulation of experience which is standardized through linguistic usage. On Skid Row, spoken language gives an accurate representation of this subculture.

The words characteristic of Skid Row may be placed into two categories: 1) agency-related words (hotels, labor offices, missions, police-jail-court), and 2) street-related words (bumming, drinking, names, places, smoking). This is not to infer that these categories limit the whole of Skid Row behavior. Rather these semantic descriptions of Skid Row are set apart from other English forms in that the latter cannot effectively relate common experience within the particular structures of this culture.

To indicate the extent of word use, each word in this chapter is preceeded by a number signifying the percentage of men who gave this definition when asked the meaning of the word. 1=90% to 100%, 2=50% to 90%, 3=10% to 50%, and 4=0% to 10%.

HOTEL WORDS
FLOP   (1) A men's cubicle hotel, or a room in a flophouse.
(2) Any place a Skid Row man sleeps.

LABOR OFFICE WORDS
GANDY DANCER   (1) A railroad worker.
SLAVE MARKET   (1) A day labor office.

MISSION WORDS

EARBEATING   (1) The hour to two hour fire-and-brimstone mission service.

MISSION STIFF   (1) A man on a mission program, or one who makes the missions every day and depends upon them for food, lodging and clothes.

NOSE DIVE   (1) Going to the front of a mission assembly, usually during a part of the service known as the altar call, to profess to the preacher one's acceptance of Jesus Christ as his personal Savior; getting saved, normally to get on a program.

SALLY   (1) The Salvation Army.

SOUP LINE   (1) A line of men in front of a mission before a service.

POLICE RELATED WORDS

BULL   (1) A policeman.

(3) A railroad detective.

(4) A male cow (sic).

BULLPEN   (1) A large cell where Skid Row prisoners are deposited to await Call Court.

BUM WAGON   (1) A patrol wagon used in arresting "drunks" on Madison Street.

CAN   (1) Jail.

(4) Toilet.

FLOATER   (1) Judge's suggestion to "get out of town."

(4) A person who travels aimlessly from town to town.

HOOKNOSE   (2) A cop with a hooked nose.

KICKOUT   (1) Getting released by the judge after one night in jail. (2) Being thrown out of some establishment.

MAKING THE BUCKET   (1) Getting arrested.

MEAT TRUCK   (1) A paddy wagon which picks up the bodies of men who die in the Skid Row hotels.

MUTT AND JEFF   (1) Two policemen, one tall, one short.

(3) Two policemen who were transferred or retired, and who are remembered for their brutality and jackrolling.

SCREW also TURNKEY   (2) A guard who locks up the prisoners in jail.

96

(4) A piece of metal.

TANK   (1) Jail.

DRINKING WORDS

BOTTLE GANG   (1) Two or more individuals drinking out of the same bottle. For the most part, any individual may partake in the affair by contributing dimes, nickels or pennies. Often, those unable to put in money are not deprived of a drink.

BUG JUICE   (3) Wine or other types of alcohol.

JUG   (1) A bottle of liquor.   (2) A bottle of wine.

MAKE A RUN   (1) To purchase a bottle of wine or something (cigarettes, food, etc.) for someone or a group.

PASSIN' THE BOTTLE   (1) Applies to the act of sharing wine in a bottle gang or with another person.

PINK LADY also SQUEEZE, CANNED HEAT   (1) A drink made of the alcohol from Sterno strained by means of a handkerchief or a cloth of some kind and then mixed with water. A good number of men on Skid Row have tried pink lady. One man remarked, "It almost killed me."

RUNNER   (1) The person who makes the run, i.e., the purchaser.

SPIDER   (2) The last amount of alcohol in a bottle. This word is in some ways a commentary on Skid Row life—a culture that needs to name the last few drops in a jug.

SWEET LUCY   (3) Wine.

WENT SOUTH   (1) When a man is given money to make a run, but disappears in the interim.

BUMMING WORDS

BEGGING AND PANHANDLING   Most answers from Skid Row men establish no difference between these words; both denote bumming.

BUMMING also STEMMING   (1) This term has multifarious levels of understanding on Skid Row. It first bears the meaning of a way of life: flopping anywhere, eating anything. A second use of this word is to beg money, food, wine, cigarettes, etc.

CHUMP CHANGE   This has the same meaning as "starter" though it has not gained as wide a currency on Skid Row.

GOT A QUARTER ON A JUG? (1) This is a question used as a way of amassing necessary funds for a bottle of wine.

MAKING A FLOP (1) Bumming or working to get money for a flop. (4) Making a mission.

STARTER (1) Small change, ultimately for a jug. A man on Skid Row can bum money for a bottle by asking others, "Can you help me out with a starter?"

NAMES OF PLACES

BUG HOUSE SQUARE (2) A park on Clark Street just north of Chicago Avenue, visited by many men from Skid Row.

HOBO JUNGLE (1) A location, usually near railroad tracks, where a few hobos will take food (which they have bummed) and prepare a make-shift stew to eat. Traditionally men stayed at hobo jungles as they "beat" their way across the country on freight trains.

SMOKING WORDS

MOTOR IS RUNNING (2) A description of a cigarette, still burning, found in the street.

SNIPE (2) A used cigarette butt.

NAMES

BINDLE STIFF (3) A man who travels carrying some personal belongings wrapped in a blanket.

CHIEF (1) A term for addressing Indians.

HOMEGUARD (3) An individual who never leaves the city.

JACKROLLER (1) A person who steals something, usually money.

TRAMP, HOBO, and BUM Most Skid Row men fail to contrast a tramp with a hobo; to them, both are persons who work and travel. The word bum is somewhat different in that it refers to a man who won't work and doesn't travel.

TABLE 8.1 SKID ROW MEN'S DEFINITIONS OF TRAMP, HOBO, AND BUM

		#
	All three same	6
17#	Tramp and hobo same	9
26%	Tramp and bum same	1
	Hobo and bum same	1

		Works	Won't Work	Travels	Doesn't Travel
		#	#	#	#
49#	TRAMP	20	7	22	0
74%	HOBO	14	6	27	2
	BUM	2	29	1	17

MISCELLANEOUS STREET WORDS

CARRYING THE BANNER   (1) Having to walk all night because one has no place to stay.

SHANK also SHIV   (2) A knife. A shank or a shiv is, for defense purposes, sometimes a necessity of life on Skid Row.

INDIAN SKID ROW WORDS

American Indians on Skid Row are not only fluent in the basic argot of the street, but incorporate other words into their lexicon, some of which are borrowed from specific tribes. Indians, and only Indians, are acquainted with these words.

HAUNTED   (1) Abandoned.

INDIAN CHAMPAGNE   (1) Cheap wine.

INDIAN DOCKS   (1) A place where only Indians sleep.

/máyktadey/   (1) White man. Literal translation is "long knife" (named after cavalry soldiers).

/lehúnji/   (1) Black man.

NEGRO SKID ROW WORDS

Older Black men on Skid Row are knowledgeable of the morphemic patterns of Skid Row, but many Blacks retain much of their dialect(s) within the sociolinguistic setting of Skid Row.

SPANISH-AMERICAN SKID ROW WORDS

Mexican Americans and Puerto Ricans on Skid Row generally group together socially and are able to adjust to Skid Row life with only minor assimilation. A language barrier helps to separate many of these individuals from other Skid Rowers except for very superficial interaction. A factor associated with this is their attitudes which direct sanctions against any member who departs from Spanish in his conversations. Many of these informants could identify only a few of the most common Skid Row terms. Spanish-speaking persons proficient in English, however, are more likely to interact with persons of other ethnic origins.

SPANISH WORD	LITERAL TRANSLATION	SKID ROW MEANING
PERRO	dog	policeman
BOTA	can	jail
LA JULIA	a woman's name	paddy wagon
HAMBO	person who steals	jackroller
HOTELUCHO	ucho is a derogatory suffix in Spanish	Skid Row hotel
WINOS	winos	men sharing wine on the street
BAGO	man who begs	Skid Row man
TRAMPOLINA	man who lives in the alley	tramp
OFFICIA DE TRABAJA	office of work	day labor office
BARA	bar	bar
CORRIDA	runner	someone who buys wine for a group
BUMBARDERO	man who asks for money on the street	bum
SERVICIO	service	mission service

Chapter IX

Conclusions

Throughout the history of Skid Row in the United States, many recommendations have been made as to what to do with those known commonly as tramps, hobos, beggars, vagrants, etc. These recommendations have been characterized by repression and deterence.

In the latter 1800's and the early 1900's, men lacking visible means of support were run out of town, arrested, placed in workhouses and labor colonies. Cities which had available lodging or shelters often gave work tests to discourage men from becoming vagrants (Sutherland, 1936). Many writers strongly advocated measures to eliminate the destitute and homeless. In 1891, respectable journals printed columns which favored the poisoning of meat given to tramps who asked for food, thus hoping to curb the tramp nuisance (W. J. Gorsuch, 1891). In 1904, Benjamin C. Marsh, unusually disturbed by the problem of vagrancy in the major cities of the United States, outlined a plan for its eradication.

> Every mission which furnishes lodging must also be induced to establish a work test.
>
> Every new applicant for public lodging is required to take a shower bath.
>
> A mendicancy squad . . . should periodically visit the lodging houses, missions, and religious shelters, and arrest inmates who cannot give a good account of themselves on charges of either drunkenness or vagrancy.

101

State farms. Every state should have a State Farm, to which vargrants should be committed and compelled to work on the farm or at some trade.

Men should be committed on an indeterminate sentence and be entitled to release on probation . . . The probationary release should be upon the condition . . . that the holder of the permit to be at liberty does not return to his former habits of vagrancy and dissipation. To be seen entering a saloon or disorderly house should be sufficient reason for recommitment to the State Farm (1904:449-451).

Edmond Kelly in his book *The Elimination of the Tramp* (1908) argued that the unemployed should be committed to labor colonies where they would be forced to work.

The introduction of labour colonies with a view to solving the tramp problem, has occupied me for some twenty years . . . I ventured to suggest that . . . every person found wandering the highways or the streets without means of support could be inexpensively provided for.

In view of the fact that the public mind is now agitated by the extent of the tramp evil in the United States and of the acute state which the problem of the unemployed is likely to reach this winter, . . . It seems incredible . . . that an evil so great should be allowed to flourish unchecked when we have at our disposal so simple, inexpensive and complete a remedy.

The present period of industrial depression is largely increasing the army of the unemployed (1908:xv-xvii).

The labour colony is . . . a home where the indigent can be cared for, provided with work, and given habits of work that, when he is capable of acquiring them, will fit him once more for social life . . . (1908:28).

Alice Solenberger, supervisor of the Central District of the Chicago Bureau of Charities, writing in 1911, proposed the following:

Each commonwealth will require a certain minimum equipment of good institutions, if it would deal effectively with all the various types of men that are on the road . . . The institution should include . . . a compulsory farm colony for the treatment of vagrants and tramps to which they should be committed on indefinite sentences and where they could be taught trades and trained in habits of work. . . . there will be little doubt but that the particular state having such laws and such an institutional equipment will effectively and permanently rid itself of tramps (1911:236).

Professor of sociology at the University of Illinois, Edward Hayes, in his *Introduction to Sociology* (1921) offers a plan for protection against tramps and vagrants.

Unless some plan of prevention is resorted to, every city has its quota of resident town bums and dead-beats; and the army of tramps, or vagrant beggars, in the United States . . . constantly numbers according to different estimates, from sixty to one hundred thousand. These people are deserters from life's responsibilities . . .

The habitual vagrant parasite when convicted . . . should be confined in the work house . . . as protection against the moral contagion and the easily concealed crimes of irresponsible vagrants (1921:183-184).

In the appendix of Nels Anderson's book *The Hobo* (1923), the Committee on Homeless Men of the Chicago Council of Social Agencies makes these recommendations:

. . . the problem of the homeless migratory worker is but an aspect of the larger problem of industry such as unemployment, seasonal work, and labor turnover.

The committee approves . . . The establishment by the municipal, state, and federal government of colonies or farms for "down and outs" in order to rehabilitate them by means of proper food, regular habits of living and regular work that will train them for lives of usefulness.

As a program of immediate action—The establishment of a Municipal Clearing House for Non-Family Men . . . The Clear-

103

ing House will maintain the following departments: . . . iii) Vocational Clinic: to provide medical, psychiatric, psychological, and social examination as a basis of treatment. iv) Records Office: to record findings of examination, . . . and to enter recommendations and results of treatment.

Treatment: Upon the basis of the preceeding examination and classification, the men will be given the following services: . . . For incorrigible vagrants and beggars for whom no constructive treatment is provided in the program for immediate action . . . commitment to the House of Correction (1923:267-272).

Donald Bogue, in his book *Skid Row in American Cities* (1963) (the result of a research project initiated and largely funded by the Urban Renewal Administration), confidently proposes that Skid Rows should be torn down.

Because it represents urban living at its worst, city planners, welfare workers, housing experts, and urban renewal administrators have realized they can not ignore the Skid Row in their city, but must consider doing something to remove it. Not only is Skid Row a physical eyesore, it is also sociologically poisonous to neighborhoods in a broad surrounding zone (1963:4).

In his concluding chapter, "Skid Row Can Be Eliminated," Bogue offers some programs for institutionalizing men on Skid Row.

5. A program of occupational rehabilitation and training to improve the employability of Skid Row men to help them become self-supporting or to upgrade their earning power.

6. A program of treatment for Skid Row alcoholics, where the persons to be treated are not willing to cooperate voluntarily, . . .

9. A plan for detection and management of men who do not want steady work and who are not handicapped but who merely use the Skid Row welfare facilities to gain a parasitic livelihood.

104

10. A program for the rehousing and possible socialization of asocial, anti-social, and semi-neurotic persons who prefer to live in isolation.

In a study prepared for the Department of Urban Renewal in 1967, sociologist Ronald Vanderkooi presented his half-way community plan for relocating residents of Skid Row.

This community would provide housing but also such community needs as restaurants and cafeterias, employment offices, religious institutions, police protection, controlled drinking facilities and other retail outlets. By being carefully planned and supervised this community would be a "half-way" facility and not a new skid row. Within it there would be a strong emphasis upon rehabilitation and the routing of individuals through personal counseling, alcoholism programs, vocational training, various medical and mental health programs, and various agencies back into more normal American communities and activities (1967:2).

It is somewhat misleading to take the recommendations out of their historical context; after all many of them were once regarded as practical solutions to eminent problems. Many of the writers believed that the ambitious could get a job and that the unemployed were lazy, irrespective of the economic problems of the country which were generally responsible for the large numbers of the unemployed. To arrest men who are out of work during times of economic crisis and high unemployment is seemingly the height of absurdity and fanaticism. However, unable to alter the economic problems, lawmakers became concerned with restraining the jobless. An example is the depression of 1893, when thousands of foot-loose unemployed, without money and often needing food, were a threat to the security of many citizens who felt helpless and feared being overrun by an "army of tramps."

Historically, the general concern of most authors was to induce the lazy to accept work. If a man was unable or unwilling to work, he was institutionalized and placed under the supervision of correctional agencies: jails, work-houses and labor colonies. Many of the

105

same recommendations and methods for detering bums and tramps are evident today although with different emphases. In the past, tramps or hobos, the result of industrialization and economic hard times, were considered lazy and immoral, and were arrested. With the past few decades there has been a general prosperity and a marked decline in the population of Skid Rows in the United States. Today the "bum" is thought of as mentally deranged and is sent to a social worker or a psychiatrist.

In summary, most authors who wrote about tramps and vagrants recommended programs designed to control, supervise, and rehabilitate these men. Rarely was any serious attention ever given to the institutions or agencies which commonly exploit the inhabitants of Skid Row.

Presently, exploitation of Skid Row men occurs within most of the Skid Row institutions, namely Urban Renewal which has demolished Skid Row buildings to provide land for development by a wealthy elite, the businesses (the most important of which are day labor offices and hotels) which seek to maximize financial gain, and the helping or correctional agencies (the police force and missions) which attempt to rehabilitate the men.

Urban Renewal often boasts about rescuing men from the deteriorated, rat-infested, fire hazardous hotels which they have destroyed. But Urban Renewal usually fails to mention that the inhabitants of the hotels that were torn down are invariably relocated to other deteriorated, rat-infested, fire hazardous buildings in the area. I doubt that tearing down the existing Skid Row for office complexes, expensive restaurants, and theatres has benefited the men. Urban Renewal's motives for eliminating Skid Row are clearly not to help suffering humanity.

Labor offices and hotels are noteworthy for bleeding Skid Row's poverty. Many of the latest model expensive luxury cars parked along the streets of Skid Row belong to hotel and day labor office owners.

Most of Skid Row's helping agencies apparently have only the noblest of intentions, and no doubt these agencies provide, for the most part, for basic material needs of many of the men. However, those interested in helping the men on Skid Row generally proceed in their work with the assumption that Skid Row is a garden of human character disorders or sin, never questioning that their knowledge of Skid Row is indicative primarily of their occupations and selective perceptions. The bureaucratic complacency of agency personnel is satisfied by convenient theories and doctrines and a substitute for understanding, friendship, and sensitivity to the men as individuals with basic human needs, wants, joys and sorrows. The destitute of Skid Row are evangelized, "psychologized" and jailed into submission, subservience, and despair. The helping agencies of Skid Row exist to help the men and, inadvertently, regulate if not punish them.

Methods for dealing with tramps and bums today are not more humane, only more subtle. Greed and prejudice are far more influential than reason in determining policies which affect men on Skid Row.

Appendix I

Research Methodology

The obstacles I encountered in this study were immense. The experience was a frustrating and time consuming ordeal. This project first took the form of reviewing the literature on Skid Row. Later, many hours were spent in the field before determining my research objectives. From the outset I planned to study the agencies and men of Madison Street Skid Row using qualitative and quantitative methods. My three years of research included renting a room in the Imperial Hotel on Madison Street and living there three months as a participant observer, and administering questionnaires to agency personnel and men of the area. The questionnaire for the men was made up of the following items:

1. Age
2. Nationality
3. Place born
4. Childhood and present religion
5. Marital status
6. Number of children
7. Do you receive some type of assistance?
8. How much?
9. How do you spend this money?
10. Do you live in the Madison Street area of Skid Row?
11. How long have you lived here?
12. Where were you living before this?
13. How long were you there?

14. Why did you come to Skid Row?
15. Place of parents' birth
16. Father's occupation(s)
17. Parents' educational background
18. How did you get along with your parents?
19. Number of brothers and sisters
20. Briefly describe your relationship with them.
21. Number of years of formal education
22. Did you dislike any aspect of your schooling?
23. What were some of your early interests or hobbies?
24. What kind of grades did you get throughout grammar school, high school, and college?
25. Have you ever had any specialized training?
26. What types of jobs have you held in your life?
27. How many days per week do you work day labor?
28. How much do you earn per day?
29. What type of work have you done?
30. Do you have any complaints about the day labor offices?
31. Have you ever taken a job as a seasonal farm laborer since you've been on Skid Row? When? Where? Type of work? What was the pay?
32. At what hotels have you stayed since you've been on Madison Street?
33. Length of stay?
34. Reasons for moving?
35. Do you feel there are any differences between Skid Row hotels?
36. What were the conditions of the washroom facilities at the hotels?
37. How often were these cleaned? How were they cleaned?
38. How often were the sheets on the beds changed?
39. Have you ever seen any insects or other pests in the hotels?
40. What type and how often?
41. Do you have any comments about any of the Skid Row hotels?

42. What bar(s) do you go to most often? Why?
43. Is there one type of liquor you tend to drink most of the time?
44. Do you have any comments about any Skid Row bars?
45. How do you feel about Skid Row police?
46. On an average, how often are you arrested per year?
47. Reasons for arrests?
48. Do you have any complaints about the police? Jail? Court?
49. What bible mission do you attend most? Why?
50. Do you have any comments about any of the bible missions on Skid Row?
51. Have you ever used any of Skid Row's pawnshops? Which ones? Why?
52. Where do you usually eat?
53. Have you ever sold your blood? Why?
54. Where did you sell it?
55. How much were you paid?
56. What are your future plans?
57. Briefly, what are your philosophies regarding life and death?

After about sixty of these questionnaires had been administered, I was convinced that a thorough study of Skid Row men using a formal questionnaire was impossible. I had talked with many men on Skid Row before preparing the questionnaire and had few problems getting informants to answer questions. Yet once I took pen and paper and began to write down responses (particularly personal answers related to their backgrounds), I became an intruder in their lives. Many of the men, after a couple of questions, would abruptly get up and walk away. Others would repeatedly ask something like, "Just why do you want to know all those things? You a cop?!" I tried to explain the purpose of my research to gain the trust of my informants, but this failed miserably. I soon discovered that bribing men with cigarettes and money for a bottle of wine was a most effective way to get interviews. I employed this approach for administering most of my questionnaires to the men. But this technique also encountered difficulties. Regularly I was confronted with opposition. For instance,

Interviewer: What's your age?

Informant: Forty-six.

Interviewer: Where were you born?

Informant: You know, I'm going to tell you something. Anytime anybody starts asking me questions, I clam up. I say where's this motherfucker come from. Cause—let me tell ya something—I met an F.B.I. guy, no I met two F.B.I. guys, one in Saint Louis, one in Chicago. I come into Chicago twenty-five years ago. That F.B.I. man took me in the fuckin' shithouse and he shook me down. Oh yeah, you better believe it. I just come from Iowa then. I'm always coming from Iowa; why I don't know. I'm gonna go back there. I'm gonna gitch you a—hey, that cunt I was working with, if I, oh, she told me all about her, oh never mind. I want to ask you a question. Answer this question. What the fuck are you doing on Skid Row?

Interviewer: Trying to research Skid Row. I—

Informant: Do you drink?

Interviewer: Uh—

Informant: Why don't you give me money for some wine?

Interviewer: First let me ask you where you were born.

Informant: Let's see your badge. You ain't got no fuckin' badge on you, don't ask me no questions. Give me seventy cents for a pint.

(I gave him the money with the stipulation that he would answer my questions.)

Interviewer: Again, where were you born?

Informant: You tell me.

Interviewer: I don't know. I'm asking you. That's why I gave you money.

Informant: Now I know you're a fuckin' detective. What are you worried about Skid Row for?

Of those informants who agreed to answer my questions, many gave answers which, I was later to learn, were inconsistent and unreliable.

While conducting this survey I had a few informants who would get so vehemently angry that they would provoke a fight with me for no other reason than I was a researcher and they were drunk. At such times, I would discuss something that did not incite them. (Perhaps I should mention that I was never physically attacked on Skid Row.) After much disappointment, I abandoned the question-naire method of studying the men on Skid Row.

From this time forward my research was concerned primarily with the existing Skid Row agencies. My efforts to research the men after this generally centered on participation. Going through ear-beatings at missions, drinking wine in bottle gangs, getting arrest-ed, flopping in cubicles and old buildings, and living with men on Skid Row as they live, were for me the most edifying part of this research. Associating with the men provided invaluable data. Many of the men's comments were actually hypotheses which prompted me to undertake further investigation.

In researching Skid Row agencies, my approach was similar. I first went through all institutions experiencing them as would a man on Skid Row. Second, after I was familiar with a particular type of agency, I assembled and administered questionnaires to the agen-cies' management and personnel. I actively encouraged infor-mants to digress from these questions and to talk in elaborate detail about any related topics that occurred to them. This proved an important means of gathering data. Third, I asked men on Skid Row for their comments and experiences regarding the agencies. Finally, in organizing and writing up my research on agencies I found some information incomplete. Several times, if I had written what first seemed plausible, such statements would have been wrong, as was demonstrated by further examination.

Although I did have a basic overall research approach, I found that each type of agency was unique and demanded special consideration. I will present a brief discussion of the methodology developed for each agency type.

Hotels

I stayed in all of the cubicle hotels and many of the other hotels on Madison Street. The dirt and stench of the hotels made this experience anything but pleasant. Although time made me tolerant of hotel conditions, I never found them entirely acceptable except for the purposes of research.

An interview which included the following questions was given to the owners and clerks of each hotel.

1. Name of hotel
2. Address
3. Number of employees
4. What is your position in the hotel?
5. What kind of work do you do in this job?
6. What is your income?
7. How long has your hotel been at its present location?
8. Give a brief history of the hotel.
9. What services do you provide for guests?
10. What is the average number of men who live in your hotel on a typical day (summer vs. winter)?

11. Age of men?	Under 30	—%
	30 to 45	—%
	45 to 60	—%
	Over 60	—%
12. Nationality of men?	Black	—%
	Indian	—%

Spanish-speaking	—%
White	—%
Other	—%

13. Length of time men stay at your hotel?

1 day to a week	—%
1 week to 1 month	—%
1 month to 6 months	—%
6 months to 1 year	—%
1 year to 3 years	—%
3 years to 10 years	—%
10 to 25 years	—%
25 years or more	—%

I had planned on interviewing the clerks and, if possible, the owners of every hotel. There were considerable difficulties involved in getting these interviews. Often the hotel personnel would have no part of my questioning. For example, I would introduce myself, "I'm doing research on Skid Row. Would you mind answering some questions for me if you're not busy? It won't take more than five or ten minutes." Clerk: "I ain't interested." I would try to be friendly, "I'd really appreciate it if you'd answer the questions. Whichever ones you don't like, don't bother to answer." Clerk: "I told you, I ain't interested. Get outa here!"

I had experiences much like this one in about ten of the hotels. If someone were uncooperative, I would simply return to the hotel to get an interview when another person was working. To my advantage, many Skid Row hotels have a large turnover of employees, as well as two shifts of workers each day.

Missions

The data in this chapter came from the directors and assistant directors of the thirteen missions found on West Madison Street Skid Row. I suffered through innumerable hours of religious services at all of the missions, and once, after "getting Jesus," was taken on an alcoholic program for a few days. This is the interview I later gave to the mission directors and their assistants.

1. Name of mission
2. Address
3. Owners
4. History of mission
5. Number of employees
6. Source(s) of income
7. What are the goals of this mission?
8. What services do you provide for the men?
9. What is the number of men who use your mission?
10. Why does your mission operate on Skid Row?
11. Why do you think men are on Skid Row?
12. How long has your mission been in operation?
13. How did you come into this organization?
14. What is your position in the mission?
15. What is your salary?
16. Age
17. Place of birth
18. Nationality
19. Marital status
20. Childhood and present religion
21. Number of children
22. Do you live on or near the Madison Skid Row area?
23. Where were your parents born?
24. What was (were) your father's occupation(s)?
25. Number of years of formal education
26. Have you had any specialized training?
27. What type of jobs have you held in your life?

In comparison with other Skid Row agencies, missions were the least difficult to research. I credit this to the mission personnel who openly lent themselves to the interviews. When each interview was over, however, I was usually put to the task of politely averting a director's verbose campaign to eradicate the errors of my life.

116

Police

I was arrested three times on Skid Row on charges of "drunk and disorderly" conduct. To prepare for this I would put on old clothes, go to a bar on Madison, drink a beer (so I would have alcohol on my breath), and go outside and wait for a paddy wagon to come along. As soon as I saw it I would begin to stagger and fall. The first time I attempted to get arrested I had no luck. I had a drink in a bar and went outside and lay down on the sidewalk as though I had passed out. It was a cold and windy winter night, and the jacket I wore was inadequate. I lay and waited on the sidewalk for an hour and a half—no paddy wagon. During that time, only a few Skid Row men walked by. A couple of them stopped to help me. Fearing I had taken sick from the cold, I gave up the attempt for the night.

I had to acquaint myself fully with police operations on Skid Row, so after receiving permission from the district commander, I rode in a squad car one night with two officers who patrol Skid Row. Next, I compiled the questionnaire for the police.

1. Age
2. Position
3. Nature of work
4. Years with the police
5. Years with present district
6. Why do you feel men are on Skid Row?
7. What services are provided by the police for Skid Rowers?
8. Do you feel anything can be done (or needs to be done) to help Skid Row?

Employment Offices

I worked out of all the employment agencies in the Madison area (working in factories, unloading trucks, washing dishes, delivering handbills, etc.), which was very slow and monotonous research. It usually required twelve hours a day, and produced only scant information.

Recent legislation intended to reform the day labor offices in Chicago has made them hesitant to give out any information. Consequently, I kept my questions for these agencies to a minimum. I list them here.

1. Number of jobs given to men per average work day?
2. Types of jobs?
3. How much do you pay?
4. What records do you keep?
5. Why do businesses use your agency?

Second-Hand Stores

To begin research of the second-hand stores I talked with forty-three men from Skid Row, asking them about their thoughts and experiences. Then I rummaged through closets and drawers at my apartment and produced some unwanted articles: an electric meat rotisserie—store bought value, $30.00; a gold ring—value, $27.00; a sterling silver bracelet—value, $20.00. I took these items to Skid Row and, with the assistance of two men from the area whom I have known since I lived on Madison, sold them at second-hand stores. Our procedure was as follows. I would go into the second-hand store first. I was to observe. One of the men would follow about fifteen seconds later with one of the items. He was to ignore me and act as if he had to sell the item for a drink. The performances of the men were nothing less than convincing. Their fine efforts brought only one dollar for the meat rotisserie, forty-five cents for the ring, and twenty-five cents for the bracelet at three different stores.

A few weeks after this, I concluded my research of the second-hand stores by asking the owners questions, such as, "What items do you sell most?" and "What are the prices for these?" Most of the other questions only angered the store owners.

Bars and Restaurants

Researching Skid Row bars and restaurants took considerable time. When I lived on Madison Street I ate most of my meals at the different Skid Row restaurants. I spent long hours drinking beer and talking with other customers in the many bars along Skid Row. For the following two and a half years, although researching other institutions, I would often go into the bars and restaurants. A productive research method for me was to offer to buy some man on Skid Row a drink or something to eat. Thus, I was able to informally discuss with the man his experiences.

Argot

The methodological task for Chapter VIII was to quantitatively formulate definitions of Skid Row words. Informants were individually told words and asked to give meanings for each. The data in this chapter are drawn from forty whites and twenty-six American Indians on Skid Row. Nineteen blacks and seventeen Spanish-speaking Americans surveyed are not included in the general analysis. These groups receive separate discussion near the end of tho chapter.

Appendix II

Supplementary Comments and Experiences of Skid Row Men

This section is made up of tape recorded conversations with fifteen men on West Madison Street Skid Row. Each paragraph represents a comment or an experience of one of these men. Although some attempt was made to organize these comments and experiences according to the chapters of this book, much of this material does not fall within the discussions of those chapters. Consequently this section is an attempt to offer a more complete understanding of the lives of men on Skid Row.

Missions

* * *

Dean Swift at Calvary Rescue Mission wanted me to stay and work for him on his program. I didn't stay. I got up in the morning and took off. I try to avoid those missions. Really—I do. It's like putting a dog in a pound—they say he's worthless after that.

* * *

The other night I was in the Helping Hand and was planning on sleeping there. But during the earbeating I reached in my pocket and I come up with a dollar and thirty-five cents I didn't know I had. Good-bye. I went and bought a pint of wine and slept out.

* * *

I got a pair of shoes on that the Salvation Army give me. The shoes are too small—seven and a half and I wear an eight and a

121

half. They told me, 'Either take the shoes or do without.' I've worn the shoes for two days. A nail in them shoes stuck me in the heal. Now it's so infected I can't hardly walk on it. Tomorrow I'll go over and get an infection shot at the clinic.

* * *

Last night at the P. G. I was washing my socks out in the shower which is against the rules. But it ain't like washing a shirt or overalls. A pair of socks ya can wash off in the shower, squeeze 'em out and hang 'em on the end of your bed. In the morning they're dry. So I'm washing my socks—I wouldn't say they were stiff but I had a hard time trying to get them off. This mission stiff followed me right to my bed and he said, 'If you do that one more time—OUT!' I said, 'Look mister, you didn't come here in a limousine. You're just like me—a tramp.'

Police

This morning I went to the Salvation Army Harbor light and got cleaned up. Auggie, a copper on the wagon said to me, 'You look nice today.' He said, 'You're shaved,' gave me a big smile and kept on going.

* * *

A month ago at the Arcade (Hotel) me and this other fellow were across the street when this cop says, 'Help us with a body over here. My buddy's got a back injury—can't lift it.' I knew why he couldn't do it. The body stunk—it was so swelled up and busted—stuff was all running out of it. They guy had been dead a couple weeks in the hotel. They had to knock the door down. If we didn't go get it then the cops woulda thrown us in the damn wagon before the day was over.

* * *

I haven't been arrested much in the last six months. Only one time. I was actually drunk that time but they didn't want me for that. They wanted what I had on me. I had just cashed a check. They cleaned me out of twenty-five dollars.

* * *

They put too damn many men in a two man cell. I've been in a cell with seventeen men in it—a two man cell. Ya have to stand up all night.

* * *

I was sober, never had a drink. I was just walking down the street. The cop said to me, 'Get in.' I said, 'I haven't even had a drink.' 'Get in.'

* * *

I was sleeping in the alley back there. This cop come up with his club—wham, right across the instep of my foot and broke it. All he had to do was shake me; I'd have woke up.

* * *

I was sitting in the lobby of the Ideal (Hotel). Two policemen got out of a meat truck and walked in. 'Couple of you guys come here. Help us carry this guy outa here.' But first the cops went in his pockets and got his money; fifteen or twenty dollars. Then we put the guy on the stretcher and carried him downstairs. They gave us enough to get a jug.

* * *

Big Red, a cop, took seventeen dollars off of me when he arrested me. The next morning I'm coming down Madison and there he was. I said, 'Look, I need some money for a drink.' I only had thirty cents on me in change. He gave me fifty cents.

* * *

I came out of the Lindy Hotel—came out about seven in the morning—go to Fisher's and buy a pint of wine. I went behind a building which is a vacant lot and drank the bottle. After that I decided to go down Madison. I looked ahead about a half block and I see the police wagon sitting in front of Rothchild's. I said I'd just better wait until those gentlemen pull around the corner which they always do and go down DesPlaines. I waited, stood on one foot, the other foot, and waited. They must be talking to somebody. I decided I was gonna walk by them. One pint of wine is just a wake-me-up. I walked on by the wagon. I had gotten about twenty yards past and they yelled, 'Hey Red. Come back here.' I walked on back there. The cop said, 'Come on. Get in.' I said, 'You tell me for what.' "Well, you're drunk.' I said, 'I beg your pardon. I'm not drunk.' 'If you're not, you're gonna get drunk, so get in.'

* * *

This morning, two policemen drove by and said, 'How ya doing today?' I told 'em, 'I'm only working on a twenty cent starter. When I'm ready I'll let you know and you can arrest me.'

* * *

If ya get picked up by the police in the morning an hour or two prior to eight o'clock, they put ya in jail for over twenty-four hours. Ya don't go with the group that's going to court that morning. If necessary they'll keep you penned up in the wagon until the men are out of court. Then they'll throw you in jail. There you go, with nothing fit to eat, ya stew in your own juice in that cell with that dirty cold concrete always half freezing. That jail house at Racine and Monroe is forever cold. In fifteen years of visiting that place there isn't once I didn't suffer. They'll put ten men in a two man cell. It's impossible to make a phone call. I went in there one time with—I was picked up with—seventy dollars. When I got out the next morning I had forty some odd dollars, which amazed me that I had any. So between the wagon and the lockup, the cops left me with more than half my money.

* * *

Every time the cops see me, even if I ain't all drunk, they pick me up and throw me in jail. I always make the work detail. Get down and scrub the whole place. Ya mop the first floor and the second floor; don't have to do the courtroom anymore. That keeps me from going before the judge which is known as J-A-I-L. Next morning when I finish working the cops'll give me a drink and turn me loose.

* * *

In Kansas City I was stretched out in the weeds—another man and myself passed out behind a billboard. We got five days apiece out of that. The sergeant of police told the judge, 'Your honor, we have no record of this man,' meaning me. He said, 'I thought you'd like to know.' The judge said, 'I always like to know, so we'll only give him five days.'

* * *

I did ten days in Louisville in what they call the J.C.J. That's the Jefferson County Jail. I'm out nine o'clock in the morning and I'm back in that night for night court. I made the mistake, I had a bus token and the first guy I approached was a well dressed colored man. I said, 'Listen will ya give me twenty cents for this?' They were a quarter. He said, 'Sure. Come with me.' How was I to know he was a plain clothesman. Walked me right down to the station. Another ten days.

*   *   *

I had three quarters. When I got arrested I put them into my socks because sometimes you get in jail and some men will rob ya. Especially in the bullpen where its like sardines in a can.

*   *   *

They took us upstairs to the bullpen at five thirty. Court isn't till nine o'clock. Ya don't even go in front of this new judge, you just walk right by—just holler 'here' when he calls your last name. Here, and that's it. He doesn't even look up.

*   *   *

Fifteen, twenty years ago you could sit on the curb all day, drink wine and unless you passed out the police didn't bother you at all. Not today.

*   *   *

Hugo, was he dirty—filthy, I mean filthy. His beard, was it ever long. These cops said, 'Hugo, get up and start marching toward Monroe Street.' He wanted to get in back of the squad. They said, 'Oh no! You crummy bastard. Walk!'

Bridewell

They made ya work. Ya got normal shifts; ya work eight hours a day, seven days a week. All the jobs are at Bridewell. They got their own power plant and everything. They make their own electricity. These trains used to come in with coal. Have to unload the coal trains and everything else.

*   *   *

They usually put me in the kitchen or as a caretaker of the cells. There were three of us. Everybody made their own bed; we swept up and mopped up and cleaned the toilets and wash bowls.

125

*   *   *

Bridewell in the city—you had two man cells. At the end of the day when you had your supper at four o'clock you went in that cell until six-thirty the next morning.

*   *   *

You get a change of uniform and a shower once a week. You're allowed to write one letter a week. It had to be to a family member, but you gave them the letter unsealed and they mailed it.

*   *   *

For meals you'd get cereal or rice, bread and coffee. At noon you'd get some conglomeration of things that'd have rice and potatoes mixed in with it. Supper was the biggest meal, but you didn't get meat more than three or four days a week. I used to trade off my meat for four or five cigarettes. If you go in there without cigarettes you're outa luck. They got a store order two days a week. If ya got money on the books you can place an order for cigarettes, canned meat, almost anything as long as you got money on the books.

*   *   *

When you're sent to Bridewell, unless you have money you're hurting for certain. One time, I went there—I've never forgotten it. I was in the south cell house and this guy was leaving. He was going to hit the bricks as they say. He saw me and he walked over to me and he said, 'Here's some matches and a full can of tobacco and papers.' That seventeen days I was set.

*   *   *

Years ago they nailed metal plates to the table at Bridewell. When they put the food in the plate and you got done eating they had men come around and all they did was just wipe it out with a rag. I've heard the Bridewell was used during the Civil War. They had prisoners there from the Confederacy.

Hotels

I've been staying at the Starr Hotel. It's the home of more cockroaches, mice, and rats than you can imagine. I took a shower there yesterday and the scum on the floor was so slippery I thought I would slip and bust my head. Finally by hanging onto the side I got myself clean.

*　　*　　*

A lot of guys get a check and pay their hotel rent, and keep the rest of the money in their pockets for food. The clerk'll cash the check to pay the rent. If you come back drunk he'll find out if ya have any money left. If you have, ya won't after that. Clerks got pass keys and'll take your money when you're asleep. If the clerk don't jackroll ya then the porter'll do it, and they'll split it. Then with no money ya have to live off the missions to eat.

*　　*　　*

In some of these flophouses a jackroller'll rent a different room for three or four nights using another name, and then keep the keys. I saw one guy get caught in the Mohawk a few years ago. He had just about as many keys as the hotel did. He could go in most any room up there.

*　　*　　*

I went up to the Aetna, got a room. It was only fifty cents a night then. Half the rooms didn't have a door; the other half had beds with no mattresses. I sent a guy to get me two fifths of wine and a bar of soap—Smiley we called him. When he came back I gave him a dollar. I knew once I got in the shower and got the clothes cleaned up it would be several hours before they dried. I shut the door and proceeded to get drunk. I slept about six—maybe seven—hours. When I woke up sure enough the clothes were dry.

*　　*　　*

I was staying at the Legion. My room was on the second floor. I had my bottle and I woke up during the night and I sat up, turned on the light and reached for my bottle, and lo and behold—just as I reach for it—ya know there's an opening between the floor and the walls—here comes a rat running through my room to the next one. He was over a foot and a half long. I'm deathly scared of rats.

*　　*　　*

I moved out of the Barton Hotel near where the Salvation Army is. Two days after, thirty-one men got killed jumping out of windows from a fire. Some guy had rubbing alcohol and run through the aisles and started a fire.

*　　*　　*

127

A night clerk at Collins—he's been dead for ten years—give me a blanket and—after midnight I'd go there—he'd let me sleep on the floor in the lobby.

* * *

I was in the Working Man's Palace one time. A white fella brought a colored guy in—it was on a Saturday night—had a whole handful of change—well I found sixty cents of it after he threw it up in the air. He tried to get this guy a room and the clerk, 'Uh-uh.' He put the kibosh on that real quick. He took all that change and threw it up in the air, and of course I was there—both hands working.

Bars

Big Sam is the day manager there. Alot of times when I'm ten or fifteen cents short, I let him know I'm short. He'll tell me, 'Oh, that's all right.' But I bring back what I owe him. It might be a few days or something.

* * *

I've known a lot of good bartenders. Years ago there was King's Paradise. You could go in with Jerry the bartender and leave your money with him. He'd say, 'All right, how much do you want per day?' Well you'd take five bucks or so. He'd always say, 'Now look it, you can come in here with your tongue hanging out after you get your fin and that's it.' And he meant it. He was very honest. In King's Paradise I worked there once—not as a bartender—on the lunch counter. I lived next door in the Lindy. The vacant lot next to the Lindy—that was the King's Paradise. So every night when I got ready to leave, Marshall on the Liquor counter would have my little libation ready. Two pints of wine and one pack of cigarettes—that was one dollar then—it was only twenty cents for cigarettes if you worked there, twenty-five cents otherwise; wine was forty, forty-five cents if you didn't work there. I'd drop my dollar and pick up my lunch bag. That was a nice place. Every Friday—what the devil was this fella's name—Larry something—if he didn't weight three hundred pounds he didn't weight two pounds. So he'd get right facing the front door. He'd be between the door and the bar. They had a bar just like in Big Rothchild's—same kind—a circular bar—a horse shoe bar I think they call them. Anyhow he'd have that card table, and for ten cents you got two slices of bread and fish. Well the fish stuck out on either side. That was a meal in itself—ten cents!

Restaurants

I can remember when you got breakfast for fifteen cents. Ya got eggs and potatoes, toast and coffee. That was back in the fifties. They had on the corner of what is now—where the Holiday Inn is— Halsted and Madison Streets—they had a Thomson's Restaurant, and coffee was a nickel. So we'd walk to the fourteen hundred block, and ya got a bag of all broken up doughnuts for eight cents. We'd double back, get our nickel coffee and the manager would come—it was a ritual—'Hmmm.' We'd be drinking their coffee and outside doughnuts. When you're short ya have to do the best ya can with the tools on hand.

*   *   *

Then there was the Chili Parlor. Ya went up to the window—for fifteen cents ya got a huge platter of chili mac—it was spaghetti with chili. If ya paid a quarter ya had better bring someone else with ya to eat—it was too much.

Reading Room

I was in the Reading Room all day yesterday—that is, all afternoon. I shaved and washed up. To dry off ya have to use newspapers. They don't supply towels. They'll give you a bucket so ya can rinse out a shirt or socks—something like that, and if ya want to use the commode ya have to go to the desk to get the toilet tissue and bring it right back when you're done. I like to listen to the radio station, and I get the news every hour, or I watch T.V. I watched the Cubs ball game yesterday. Some fellas just go there just to take a nap. When they get caught, Pat wakes them up. Then they have about twenty more minutes to catch another nap. After usually about the third time he'll tell 'em, 'Get some air.' If ya even look like you had a drink ya just don't get in.

Appendix II

The Public Bath House

The bath house is open from two to four for the fellas on the street. The water is always running. They keep it warm. They don't try to freeze ya out so ya'll leave in a hurry.

Starr and Garter Theatre

Jackrollers used to go in there and rob the drunks who were sleeping. Usually the guy'd be sitting behind you going in your pockets, after your money. If you squawked they'd turn the lights on and call the police. Both of you liable to go to jail though.

Barrels

Go to Fulton Market anytime during the week except Saturday and Sunday. I carry a meat hook for breaking holes and use either wire or rope to tie barrels together. For the rim tops ya get twenty-five cents apiece; for the ones without 'em ya get a quarter for two. Then ya walk down to Peterson's on Green and Monroe, set them down. He comes out and pays you. He then cleans them and renovates them and then resells them. Those barrels are always in high demand. On a good day I'll find as many as twelve barrels. Most days I'll only get about seven barrels. From Peterson's we head right to Vogt's and get a fifth or a pint.

Bottle Collection Agency

Smoky runs the bottle collection agency.

You get a half cent for a bottle. It has to be clear—in other words no colored bottles, like green or brown. And he doesn't pay ya in cash—he pays ya in wine. That way he has ya at the end of the leash at all times. To get paid ya have to take the rings off the bottle with a can opener or something and put the bottle in a case. A case is fifteen cents; actually it's twelve cents because it's twenty-four bottles at a half a cent but he gives ya the benefit of the difference. What he does is he stores them in the back of his place there. When he gets a truck load he calls the bottle company and they take the bottles.

Elections

On election day you'll never see a wagon until six o'clock at night when the polls close. You'll see squad cars but no wagons. They want every vote they can get, the Democrats. Skid Row is the strongest Democratic ward in the whole city.

*　　*　　*

One time I was over to the Mills (Hotel). I was registered there. I knew Kelly the committeeman. So, I says, 'I'm going in and vote.' He said, 'Why hell yes, you better; you're registered.' I went in; the fella in front of me he was drunk. He voted and when he came out he said, 'Do I get a dollar?' They said, 'How did you vote?' 'I voted straight Republican.' They said, 'Then see your Republican committeeman.'

*　　*　　*

When I go in the booth I'll tell the man, 'You pull the lever—make it straight Democrat.' The guy comes in with you and closes the curtain. He gives you a dollar or two—for an off election one dollar; for Mayor Daley or a presidential election two dollars.

*　　*　　*

They had quite a stink a few years ago. They were using names of fellas who must have died in the Spanish American War. About five or six years ago there was a scandal; they called it the wine election. They were giving pints of wine depending how you voted. It came out in the newspaper. That's one thing about this ward: the boys go all out for that Democratic party. The ward committeeman works for the city in the Sewer Department. He really goes out and gets the votes.

131

Bookies

Ya get a scratch sheet for fifty cents at the Starr Hotel. Then all ya do is bang on the back door of a building near the Lindy. They don't let you in. They open the door; you just give them the first name or a code name of whoever's placing the bet, the horse, and post time and money. They wouldn't take a bet from someone unless they know ya on the street. They operate anytime the tracks are open. This cabdriver gives me money all the time. He'll give me as much as twenty bucks; he knows I won't go south. I go back the next day and he tells me if he won or anything. He won the daily double three weeks ago and guess what I got. A ten dollar bill. There's alot of disabled veterans down here drawing good money. Those guys place alot of bets. Like Wingy; he bets every day.

Bootleggers

When taverns close, then the bootlegger comes out. If someone wants a bottle he's going to have to pay the dollar and a half, or wait until seven o'clock the next morning—twelve o'clock on Sunday. Everybody knows just who to go to like Gunner and Joe. Joe was the boss and Gunner worked for him. Ya rapped on the door and ya handed him the money with one hand and he handed you the pint from the other.

*   *   *

Fifteen years ago in a bar that used to be where the Victory Club is now, ya went in there, seventy cents a pint for bootleg wine. There was no label on it, no seal. It was homemade wine. They gave ya a glass. Just sat down at a booth or at a table. Poured out your own drinks. It was good wine. I drank quite a bit of that.

Wall Street Journal

This reporter from the Wall Street Journal interviewed twenty guys at Catholic Charities. He thought I had the most interesting story. I had two years of college—got kicked out of the University of

Illinois at Champaign-Urbana on account of drinking. I also had a trial with the St. Louis Cardinals. Wally Rutgers used to play third base for the St. Louis Cardinals—said, 'Tom, you got a million dollar arm and a ten cent brain.' I used to go out and get drunk before I'd pitch the next day. I was strictly a fast ball left hander. I was a sergeant in the Marines in the war. The only man in my squad that didn't get killed. I don't know why I'm still alive. We were setting up an ammunition dump and we were hit. My sister owns a big beauty shop—she's got twenty employees. I come down after that article. She saw me and said, 'I want you to come back in this back room! I want to show you something.' She's got quite a temper and was she mad. I didn't think they'd use my name or my picture on the Wall Street Journal. All he gave me was a dollar and had me sign a release.

Railroads

I knew a guy who got his legs chopped off. His name was Garret. He tried to catch a freight and as he got ahold of the side, it went too fast for him. Maybe he was a little drunk also—lost both legs. I never get on a moving freight if I'd been drinking. I may be drunk when I get off of it, but I wouldn't take a drink before.

* * *

I'd ask the switchman in the yard which train was going out next. I'd find an empty boxcar. After awhile I could look at the tags they had on the side of the boxcars and know where it was going.

* * *

Usually railroad bulls if they catch ya will chase you outa the yard. Alot of guys I know have been beat up by thom. They used to lock ya up and call the policemen and the police'd put you in jail sometimes for as long as six months. I got run outa the yards at Kansas City. I know one guy who got beat up so bad he had to have a stomach operation, cause he sneaked back right after they chased him outa the yard. I always wait two or three days before I try again. He went right back in the yards. The bull beat him up a second time.

Hobo Jungles

A small town in Southern Illinois on the Mississippi River—you go down there, and there's a jungle. They got pots and pans hanging up on the trees, so ya can cook up. The town's a transfer point for the freight trains. We go into town—we'd bum this grocery store and that grocery store and another grocery store—get cabbage 'n carrots, or anything—salt 'n' pepper for seasoning—and we go down in the jungle and cook up. They had a razor there if ya wanted to shave. But put it back. They had fishing poles there. Ya go out 'n' fish on the Mississippi River; catch a fish, take 'em in, fry 'em up in the skillet. But when you're done, clean the skillet out, and hang it back up for the next tramp. You use a plate and knives and forks, spoons and a cup, you clean it.

Sterno

It's cheap; you can take one thirty-five cent can of Sterno, put it in a cloth, then squeeze the alcohol out of it. Add water and it'll make a quart. It amounts to about forty percent alcohol. Straight it's like a hundred and ninety proof alcohol. I wouldn't take a drink of that straight. My god—I'm crazy, but I'm not that crazy. Only thing—when ya drink Sterno, ya got to have a grocery store close by cause ya got to eat something. It makes ya hungry.

Street

One time I was on Michigan Avenue late at night—summer time. This woman was window shopping. She saw me pick up a cigarette butt. She was watching me and I didn't know it. So she called me over. 'Do you smoke those?' I could have given her a sarcastic answer and told her, 'No, it's my hobby. I've got a basement full of them.' But I didn't. I said, 'Yes, I'm hard up.' So she took out a pack of Philip Morris—there were two or three missing out of it I suppose. I thanked her and started to walk away. 'Oh, just a minute,' she said.

'When did you eat last?' 'I think it was yesterday morning.' She gave me two dollars. I thanked her and took off down the street.

* * *

Alot of times Matt would say—we'd be sitting on the curb by the old White Palace—he'd come over and he'd say, 'I suppose ya want to buy a bottle.' 'Oh yes Matt, by all means.' So I'd make the run. Always went to Big Rothchild's because ya got the two cigarettes there.

* * *

Ya'd be surprised at the number of people that come through Skid Row in their cars with the back window down, someone sitting in the back of the car with a camera. Now one time a guy brought a whole case of wine out—it was open—you ought to see them fellas grabbing that stuff. I was one of 'em. Meanwhile he was really burning up the film.

* * *

Just like a fella said—it was on a Saturday. A big sight seeing bus was there and he hollered out to them. He said, 'Yeah, that's it, look at the monkeys. I came down here five years ago to do the same thing and now I'm one.'

* * *

A man I know, he was a pharmacist by trade. His name was Val Rieght. He lived in St. Louis. He said, 'I just got up that one morning and I figured this is it.' So he started out to work and he simply got on a bus—a Greyhound—and came to Chicago instead of going to work. And that was twenty-two years ago. He's still on Madison Street.

* * *

I thought I had some bugs on me. I took that shirt off. I took that damn thing off and throwed it away. When you're down on Skid Row ya expect to get bugs, but if ya keep them it's your own fault. Tomorrow when my check gets here, I'm gonna buy complete new clothes at 1001 and take a good hot bath. I live from check to check. Maybe I'll pay a week's room rent or maybe I'll pay two weeks room rent. When the room rent's due I have to go sleep out and make the missions. This time I'm gonna play it smart. I get a hundred sixty-one fifty. And I can pay a month's room rent. Last month, I didn't

135

have enough sense to pay a month's flop. I paid a week's flop; now I'm sleeping in the alley.

* * *

I was sleeping in a building near Jackson and Van Buren. I woke up in the morning, Jack Matson that I knew real well said, 'I've got your half pint here. I thought I'd hold it so nobody'd grab it from ya.' I had finished off half a pint before I went to sleep. I had three or four cigarettes, so I gave him one and we each smoked one. We killed the half pint and then picked up our papers and cigarette butts and took off. Cause the night watchman when he goes home he comes through the factory door and through where we sleep. He'll say, 'All right, six o'clock, time to go.'

* * *

I can always get a few cigarettes or even a cigar at the bus stops or under the elevated stations downtown. They don't allow smoking on C.T.A. buses or trains. So a man'll throw away his cigarette before he gets on a bus or a train.

* * *

Down here, don't even have to know anybody. A guy comes up to ya and he says, 'How much you got on a drink?' 'I got a starter— forty cents.' 'You got a quarter, dime, nickel? Let's get a jug.'

* * *

I come in after making a day's pay and get drunk. Some jack-rollers took all the money I had left on me and run off with it. I didn't say nothing.

* * *

O'Flaherty come up to me. He says, 'Keith, I got ten dollars of your money.' 'Of my money?' 'Yeah, a few days ago you told me to hold it for ya. You think I'm a jackroller?' I said, 'You keep the ten dollars and you take me out and buy me a drink.'

Appendix III

Maps of Skid Row

The maps herein are numbered so that each directly aligned north and south block along Madison Street Skid Row was taken as one unit. Each unit going east to west is ascribed a number 1 through 15. Any blocks north or south of these central units where there are existing Skid Row buildings are also paired into units and given subscripts of s(south) and n(north) while retaining the section number.

KEY TO MAPS

This key remains constant for all the following maps.

A) Bar
B) Employment Agency
C) Hotel
D) Mission
E) Second-Hand or Clothing Store
TYPE OF INSTITUTION   F) Police
OCCUPYING BUILDING   G) Short-Order Restaurant
H) Vacant Lot or Parking Lot
I) Other (not related to needs of
    Skid Row men)
i-e) Other (almost exclusively utilized
    by Skid Row men)
i-s) Other (utilized somewhat by
    Skid Row men)
i-?) Other (not known to what extent
    used by Skid Row men)
J) Unknown
K) Apartment (usually a room)

I) Level 1
II) Level 2
BUILDING LEVEL   III) Level 3
IV) Level 4
V) Level 5
VI) Level 6

*   Moved or went out of business—building now vacant.
(*) Moved or went out of business within the last two years—building now
    vacant.
(A) Up to two years ago a bar had occupied this building.
(B) Up to two years ago an employment agency had occupied this building.
    Etc. . . .

▨ Building was demolished within the last two years.

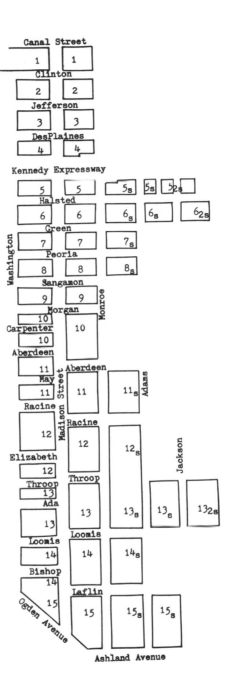

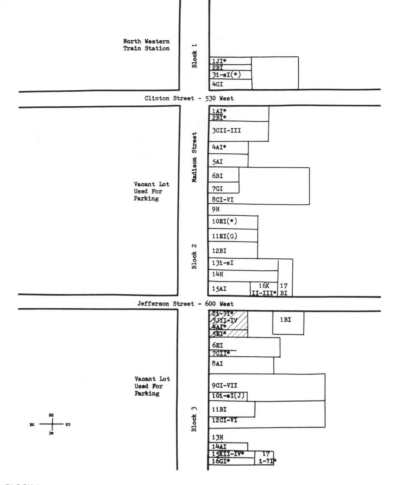

North Western
Train Station

Block 1

Clinton Street - 530 West

Madison Street

Vacant Lot
Used For
Parking

Block 2

Jefferson Street - 600 West

Vacant Lot
Used For
Parking

Block 3

BLOCK 1

1. Unknown
2. Standard Contracting
3. Drug Store
4. LaSalle Restaurant

BLOCK 2

1. Bar
2. Flash Man Inc.
3. New Breslin Hotel
4. Bar
5. Working Man's Exchange
6. Ace Labor
7. Lindy Grill
8. Lindy Hotel
9. Parking Lot
10. Johnny's Trading Post
11. Madison Second-Hand Store
12. Chicago Help Unlimited
13. Delicatessen
14. Parking Lot
15. Bar

16. Apartment rooms
17. "We hire camp cooks and helpers"

BLOCK 3

1. Ill. State Employment Service
2. Grocery and delicatessen
3. Unknown business
4. Bar
5. The Last Chance Store
6. Sam's General Merchandise
7. Freemont Hotel
8. Sid's Junction
9. Starr Hotel
10. Starr Hotel Recreation Room
11. "Need Men For Trade Shows"
12. Working Man's Palace
13. Vacant Lot
14. Rothchild's Cut Rate Liquor
15. Apartments
16. White Palace Grill
17. Barber Shop

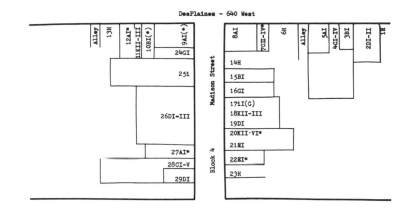

DesPlaines - 640 West

Kennedy Expressway

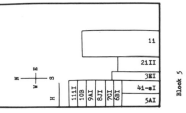

BLOCK 4

1. Parking Lot
2. Chicago United Gospel Mission
3. Milwaukee Road Track Labor
4. Legion Hotel
5. Legion Tavern
6. Parking Lot
7. Hotel
8. Rothchild's Bar
9. Bar
10. "Men Wanted—Day Labor"
11. Apartment Rooms
12. Bar
13. Parking Lot
14. Vacant Lot
15. Better Helpers
16. B&J Restaurant
17. Urban Renewal Office
18. Apartment Rooms
19. Salvation Army Clinic
20. Apartment Rooms
21. 1001 Store
22. Second Hand Store

23. Urban Renewal Parking
24. Major Grill
25. Standard Store Fixtures
26. Salvation Army Harbor Light Center
27. Bar
28. Major Hotel
29. Salvation Army Out-Patient Clinic

BLOCK 4[n]

1. Holy Cross Mission (not shown on buildings map)

BLOCK 5

1. Other
2. State of Ill. Mental Health Offices
3. Men's Clothing Store
4. Drug Store
5. 740 Liquor Store
6. Lake Shore Labor
7. Quick Lunch
8. Unknown
9. Nancy's Bar
10. "Workers Hired"
11. Midwest Cash Register

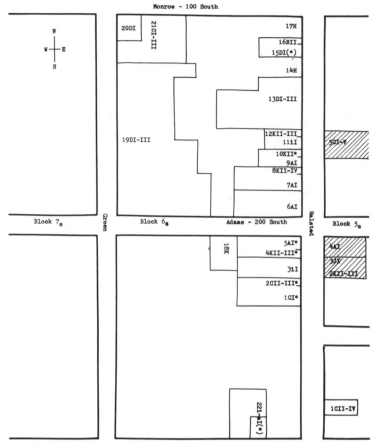

Monroe - 100 South

N
W   E
S

20DI 21CI-III

17H
16BII
15DI(*)
14H
13DI-III

19DI-III

12KII-III
11II
10KII*
9AI
8KII-IV
7AI
6AI

5CI-V

Green

Block 7₅

Block 6₅

Adams - 200 South

Halsted

Block 5₅

18K

5AI*
4KII-III*
3II
2CII-III*
1GI*

4AI
3II
2KII-III

221→II(*)

1CII-IV

Jackson - 300 South

BLOCK 5ˢ
1. New Albany Hotel
2. Apartment Rooms
3. Unknown Business
4. Bar
5. Systems Hotel

BLOCK 6ˢ
1. Edith's Restaurant
2. The New Victoria Hotel
3. Supply Store
4. Apartment Rooms
5. Bar
6. Adam's Liquor Mart
7. San Antonio Rose Tavern
8. Apartment Rooms
9. The H-Monroe Tavern
10. Apartment Rooms

11. Concession Machines
12. Apartment Rooms
13. Chicago Christian Industrial League
    Furniture Mart
14. Parking
15. St. Joseph Liberal Mission
16. Louis Bazlakis Employment Agency
17. Truck Parking
18. Apartment Rooms
19. Chicago Christian Industrial League
    Budget Store
20. West Side Rescue Mission
21. Chicago Mills Hotels
22. Blood Donor Agency

BLOCK 6₂s
1. The Standard Hotel
   (not shown on buildings map)

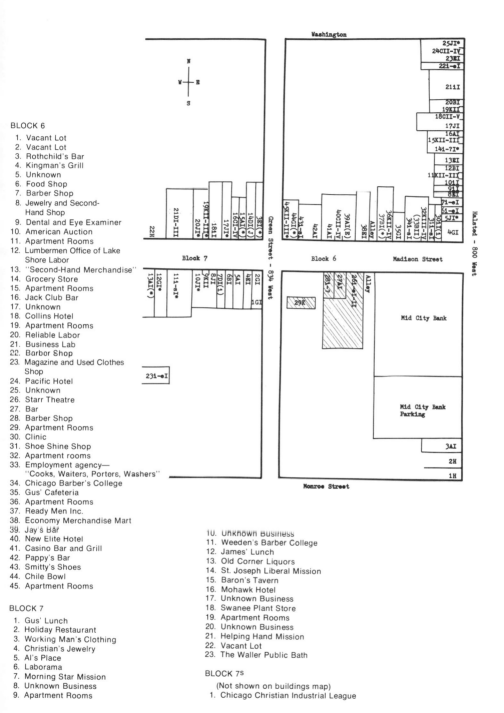

BLOCK 6

1. Vacant Lot
2. Vacant Lot
3. Rothchild's Bar
4. Kingman's Grill
5. Unknown
6. Food Shop
7. Barber Shop
8. Jewelry and Second-Hand Shop
9. Dental and Eye Examiner
10. American Auction
11. Apartment Rooms
12. Lumbermen Office of Lake Shore Labor
13. "Second-Hand Merchandise"
14. Grocery Store
15. Apartment Rooms
16. Jack Club Bar
17. Unknown
18. Collins Hotel
19. Apartment Rooms
20. Reliable Labor
21. Business Lab
22. Barber Shop
23. Magazine and Used Clothes Shop
24. Pacific Hotel
25. Unknown
26. Starr Theatre
27. Bar
28. Barber Shop
29. Apartment Rooms
30. Clinic
31. Shoe Shine Shop
32. Apartment rooms
33. Employment agency— "Cooks, Waiters, Porters, Washers"
34. Chicago Barber's College
35. Gus' Cafeteria
36. Apartment Rooms
37. Ready Men Inc.
38. Economy Merchandise Mart
39. Jay's Bar
40. New Elite Hotel
41. Casino Bar and Grill
42. Pappy's Bar
43. Smitty's Shoes
44. Chile Bowl
45. Apartment Rooms

BLOCK 7

1. Gus' Lunch
2. Holiday Restaurant
3. Working Man's Clothing
4. Christian's Jewelry
5. Al's Place
6. Laborama
7. Morning Star Mission
8. Unknown Business
9. Apartment Rooms
10. Unknown Business
11. Weeden's Barber College
12. James' Lunch
13. Old Corner Liquors
14. St. Joseph Liberal Mission
15. Baron's Tavern
16. Mohawk Hotel
17. Unknown Business
18. Swanee Plant Store
19. Apartment Rooms
20. Unknown Business
21. Helping Hand Mission
22. Vacant Lot
23. The Waller Public Bath

BLOCK 7s

(Not shown on buildings map)
1. Chicago Christian Industrial League

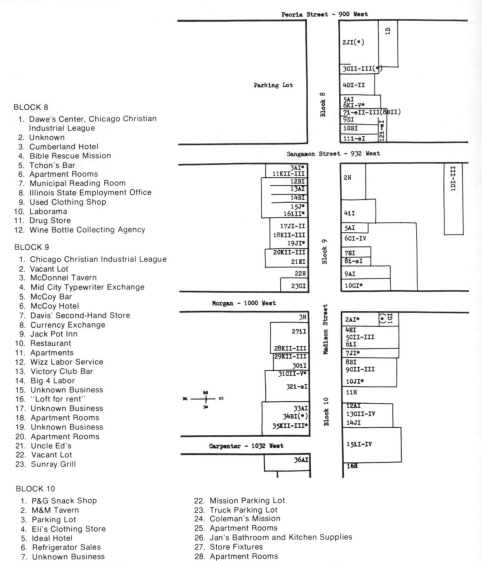

BLOCK 8

1. Dawe's Center, Chicago Christian Industrial League
2. Unknown
3. Cumberland Hotel
4. Bible Rescue Mission
5. Tchon's Bar
6. Apartment Rooms
7. Municipal Reading Room
8. Illinois State Employment Office
9. Used Clothing Shop
10. Laborama
11. Drug Store
12. Wine Bottle Collecting Agency

BLOCK 9

1. Chicago Christian Industrial League
2. Vacant Lot
3. McDonnel Tavern
4. Mid City Typewriter Exchange
5. McCoy Bar
6. McCoy Hotel
7. Davis' Second-Hand Store
8. Currency Exchange
9. Jack Pot Inn
10. Restaurant
11. Apartments
12. Wizz Labor Service
13. Victory Club Bar
14. Big 4 Labor
15. Unknown Business
16. "Loft for rent"
17. Unknown Business
18. Apartment Rooms
19. Unknown Business
20. Apartment Rooms
21. Uncle Ed's
22. Vacant Lot
23. Sunray Grill

BLOCK 10

1. P&G Snack Shop
2. M&M Tavern
3. Parking Lot
4. Eli's Clothing Store
5. Ideal Hotel
6. Refrigerator Sales
7. Unknown Business
8. "Men Wanted-Daily Pay"
9. The Arcade Hotel
10. Unknown Business
11. Parking Lot
12. Eisen's Log Cabin
13. Imperial Hotel
14. Unknown Business
15. Importing Business
16. Vacant Lot
17. Bar
18. Mexican Village Bar
19. Apartment Rooms
20. Sprague Labor
21. Olive Branch Mission
22. Mission Parking Lot
23. Truck Parking Lot
24. Coleman's Mission
25. Apartment Rooms
26. Jan's Bathroom and Kitchen Supplies
27. Store Fixtures
28. Apartment Rooms
29. Apartment Rooms
30. Paint Store
31. Grange Hotel
32. Railroad Salvage Store
33. The 1020 Club
34. Day Labor Office
35. Apartment Rooms
36. Phil's Pub
37. Herzog Store Fixtures
38. International Neon Products
39. Vacant Lot
40. Vacant Lot
41. Apartments
42. Apartments

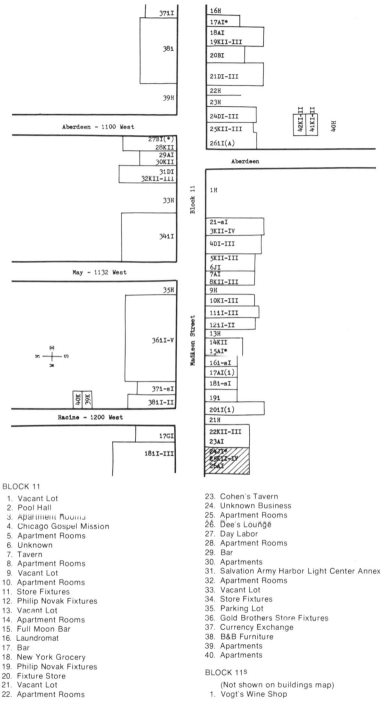

BLOCK 11

1. Vacant Lot
2. Pool Hall
3. Apartment Rooms
4. Chicago Gospel Mission
5. Apartment Rooms
6. Unknown
7. Tavern
8. Apartment Rooms
9. Vacant Lot
10. Apartment Rooms
11. Store Fixtures
12. Philip Novak Fixtures
13. Vacant Lot
14. Apartment Rooms
15. Full Moon Bar
16. Laundromat
17. Bar
18. New York Grocery
19. Philip Novak Fixtures
20. Fixture Store
21. Vacant Lot
22. Apartment Rooms

23. Cohen's Tavern
24. Unknown Business
25. Apartment Rooms
26. Dee's Lounge
27. Day Labor
28. Apartment Rooms
29. Bar
30. Apartments
31. Salvation Army Harbor Light Center Annex
32. Apartment Rooms
33. Vacant Lot
34. Store Fixtures
35. Parking Lot
36. Gold Brothers Store Fixtures
37. Currency Exchange
38. B&B Furniture
39. Apartments
40. Apartments

BLOCK 11s

(Not shown on buildings map)
1. Vogt's Wine Shop

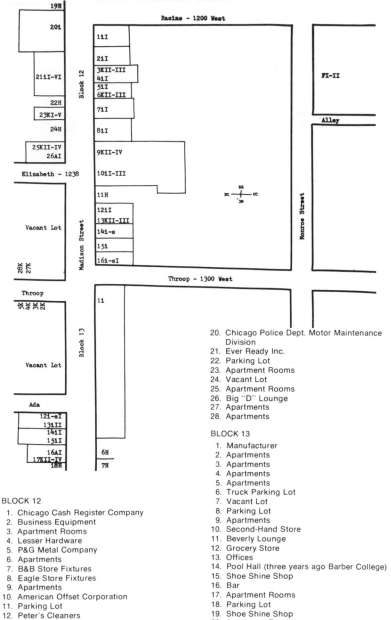

BLOCK 12

1. Chicago Cash Register Company
2. Business Equipment
3. Apartment Rooms
4. Lesser Hardware
5. P&G Metal Company
6. Apartments
7. B&B Store Fixtures
8. Eagle Store Fixtures
9. Apartments
10. American Offset Corporation
11. Parking Lot
12. Peter's Cleaners
13. Apartments
14. Throop Street Medical Center
   (Centro Medico)
15. Store Fixtures
16. Drug Store
17. Stop and Eat Grill
18. Footlik Brothers General Store Equipment
19. Parking Lot

20. Chicago Police Dept. Motor Maintenance Division
21. Ever Ready Inc.
22. Parking Lot
23. Apartment Rooms
24. Vacant Lot
25. Apartment Rooms
26. Big "D" Lounge
27. Apartments
28. Apartments

BLOCK 13

1. Manufacturer
2. Apartments
3. Apartments
4. Apartments
5. Apartments
6. Truck Parking Lot
7. Vacant Lot
8. Parking Lot
9. Apartments
10. Second-Hand Store
11. Beverly Lounge
12. Grocery Store
13. Offices
14. Pool Hall (three years ago Barber College)
15. Shoe Shine Shop
16. Bar
17. Apartment Rooms
18. Parking Lot
19. Shoe Shine Shop
20. Apartment Rooms
21. The Pretty Girl Bar
22. Gold Store Fixtures
23. Parking Lot

BLOCK 13²ˢ (Not shown on buildings map)
Bar
Burton House Hotel

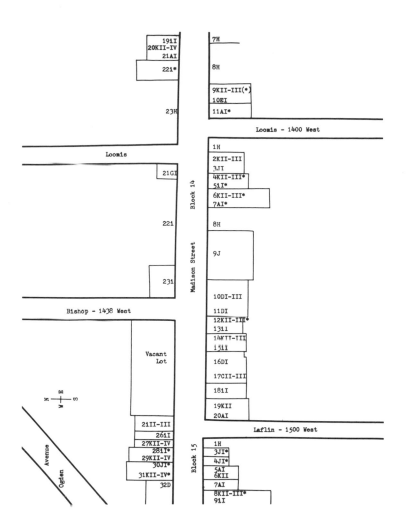

BLOCK 14

1. Vacant Lot
2. Apartments
3. Unknown Business
4. Apartments
5. Store Fixtures
6. Apartments
7. Bar
8. Vacant Lot
9. Unknown Business
10. Calvary Rescue Army Mission
11. Calvary Rescue Army Mission Resale Store
12. Apartment Rooms

13. Herman's Hardware and Paint
14. Apartment Rooms
15. Madison Towing Service
16. Calvary Rescue Mission Resale Store
17. Sylvian Hotel
18. F&G Upholstery Shop
19. Apartment Rooms
20. Kaplan Brothers Cut Rate Food and Liquor
21. Palace Grill Sandwich Shop
22. A&A Used Cars
23. "Chicken Bar-B-Q" Drive In

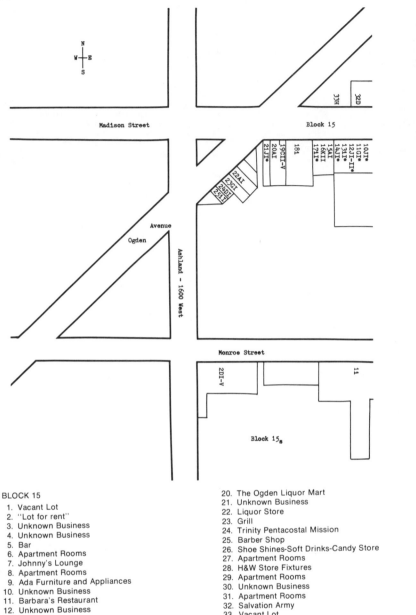

BLOCK 15

1. Vacant Lot
2. "Lot for rent"
3. Unknown Business
4. Unknown Business
5. Bar
6. Apartment Rooms
7. Johnny's Lounge
8. Apartment Rooms
9. Ada Furniture and Appliances
10. Unknown Business
11. Barbara's Restaurant
12. Unknown Business
13. Barber Shop
14. Unknown Business
15. Bull's Wild West Bar
16. Apartment Rooms
17. C&J Resale Furniture
18. Wall's Discount Department Store
19. The New Ogden Hotel
20. The Ogden Liquor Mart
21. Unknown Business
22. Liquor Store
23. Grill
24. Trinity Pentacostal Mission
25. Barber Shop
26. Shoe Shines-Soft Drinks-Candy Store
27. Apartment Rooms
28. H&W Store Fixtures
29. Apartment Rooms
30. Unknown Business
31. Apartment Rooms
32. Salvation Army
33. Vacant Lot

BLOCK 15^S

1. YMCA Rooms
2. Salvation Army Half-way House
3. Cathedral Shelter (not shown on buildings map)

References

Anderson, Nels.
    1923   *The Hobo: The Sociology of the Homeless Man*. Chicago: University of
Chicago Press.
    1940   *Men On The Move*. Chicago: University of Chicago Press.

Berger, Peter L.
    1961   *The Noise of Solemn Assemblies*. New York: Doubleday & Company, Inc.

Bogue, Donald.
    1963   *Skid Row in American Cities*. Chicago Community and Family Study Center. University of Chicago Press.

Flynt, Josiah.
    1899   *Tramping With Tramps*. New York: The Century Company.

Gorsuch, William J.
    1891   *The Tramp As a Social Factor*. Hartford: Press of Clark and Smith.

Hayes, Edward C.
    1921   *Introduction To The Study of Sociology*. New York: D. Appleton and Company.

References

James, Howard.
 1868 *The Plague of Beggars: A Dissuasive From Indiscriminate Almsgiving*. London: Henry Renshaw.

Keil, Charles.
 1966 *Urban Blues*. Chicago: University of Chicago Press.

Kelly, Edmond.
 1908 *The Elimination of the Tramp*. New York: G.P. Putnam's Sons.

Kemp, Harry.
 1922 *Tramping On Life*. New York: Garden City Publishing Company, Inc.

London, Jack.
 1907 *The Road*. New York: Macmillan.

Longstreet, Stephen.
 1973 *Chicago 1860-1919*. New York: David McKay Company, Inc.

Marsh, Benjamin C.
 1904 "Causes of Vagrancy and Methods of Eradication." *The Annals of the American Academy of Political and Social Science* 23 (May): 445-456.

Newman, Gerald S.
 1961 *The Homeless Man on Skid Row*. Chicago Tenants' Relocation Bureau.

Royko, Mike.
 1971 *Boss: Richard J. Daley of Chicago*. New York: Signet Books.

Rubington, Earl, and Martin S. Weinberg.
 1968 *Deviance, The Interactionist Perspective*. New York: Macmillan.

Solenberger, Alice W.
 1911 *One Thousand Homeless Men*. New York: Russell Sage Foundation.

References

Spicer, Edward.
1970 "Patrons of the Poor." *Human Organization* 29 (Spring): 12-19.

Spradley, James P.
1970 *You Owe Yourself A Drunk: An Ethnography of Urban Nomads*. Boston: Little Brown.

Sutherland, Edwin H.
1936 *Twenty Thousand Homeless Men*. Chicago: J.B. Lippincott Company.

Tully, Jim.
1924 *Beggars of Life*. New York: Grosset and Dunlap.

Vanderkooi, Ronald C.
1967 *Relocating West Madison "Skid Row" Residents: A Study of the Problem, With Recommendations*. A report prepared for the Chicago Department of Urban Renewal.
1968 *Skid Row: Analysis of a Deviant Social System*. Center for Urban Studies, University of Illinois.

Wallace, Samuel.
1968 *Skid Row As A Way Of Life*. New York: Harper & Row.

Wendt, Lloyd, and Herman Kogan.
1943 *Lords of the Levee*. New York: The Bobbs-Merrill Company.

Wiseman, Jacqueline P.
1970 *Stations of the Lost: The Treatment of Skid Row Alcoholics*. New Jersey: Prentice-Hall Inc.

Index

Index

154